# Sifting Through the Ashes

## Finding Beauty, Peace, Love, and Strength through Trauma

By **Darla Gale**,
Licensed Marriage and Family Therapist (LMFT)

AND

**Alice Rodriguez**,
Licensed Professional Clinical Counselor (LPCC)

DGC
PUBLISHING

Published by DGC Publishing. 6135 King Road, Suite D, Loomis CA 95650. Contact us at (916) 676-7405 or darlagalecounseling@gmail.com. To learn more about Heartstrings Counseling, the 501 (c) 3 Nonprofit Agency that this book is referencing, go to www.HeartstringsCounseling.org.

## DISCLAIMER AND/OR LEGAL NOTICES

While all attempts have been made to verify information provided in this book and its ancillary materials, neither the authors nor publisher assumes any responsibility for errors, inaccuracies, or omissions and are not responsible for any financial loss by the reader in any manner. Any slights of people or organizations are unintentional. If advice concerning legal, psychological, or related matters is needed, the services of a qualified professional should be sought. The content is not intended to be a substitute for professional advice, diagnosis, or treatment. Neither the authors nor the publisher are engaged in rendering professional advice or services to the individual reader. Neither the authors nor the publisher shall be liable or responsible for any loss or damage allegedly arising from any information or suggestion in this book. Always seek the advice of your mental health professional or other qualified health provider with any questions you may have regarding your condition. Never delay in seeking professional advice because of something you have read in this book.

The work depicts actual events in the lives of the survivors. While all persons within are actual individuals, names and identifying characteristics have been changed to respect their privacy. Permission was obtained by each individual whose story was told.

ISBN: 978-0-578-99951-7

Printed in the United States of America

# DEDICATION

This book is dedicated to those whose lives were forever changed by the tragedy of November 8, 2018, in Butte County, California and beyond. You have been through a huge ordeal and trauma, and we're dedicated to your healing journey.

To the First Responders and Emergency Personnel for their bravery and dedication to the service of others. Without your hard work and heroic efforts, these stories may not have even been possible.

This book is also dedicated to anyone who struggles with trauma and wants to find their own inner thriver: we believe in you and support you in your journey to healing.

# ACKNOWLEDGMENTS

We would like to thank so many important people who helped make this book what it is.

To the many Camp Fire Survivors and Thrivers for their courage and willingness to share their stories. We know it is important for your voices to be heard so that others can heal. We are grateful for your contributions.

To the First Responders and Emergency Personnel who contributed their stories, which added an additional laycr to this book.

To Noah Berger for allowing us to use his moving photography for the cover of this book. Noah is a freelance photographer based out of San Francisco.

To Katrina Sawa for her guidance, expertise, and never-ending support in the creation of this book. Without her, this book would have never happened. Katrina is a business coach and mentor who has helped countless entrepreneurs reach for the stars.

To Heather Moore for her knowledge, insights, and clinical contributions to this book. Heather is a licensed therapist and life coach who has helped people across the country break free from limiting ancestral trauma and faulty internal programming.

To Mandy Feder-Sawyer for her contributions throughout this book. Mandy is a freelancer and contributor with several publications including the Chico/Sacramento/Reno News & Review, National Geographic online and Entrepreneur Magazine.

To Janet Beck for her contributions in editing, proofreading, and her attention to detail in finalizing this book. Janet has been our "emotional support human" on this journey.

To Beverly Ehrman for her amazing editing and communication skills. We are so grateful for her contribution and expertise which helped to create a polished manuscript. Beverly is a full-time freelance editor of fiction and nonfiction.

To the Heartstrings Counseling therapists for their hard work and dedication to the survivors of the Camp Fire and for providing thousands of sessions to those affected by the devastation.

And lastly, to our husbands Jeff Gale and Randy Rodriguez, for their love and encouragement as we navigated the creation of this book and for the endless weekends they spent without us as we met with and supported the fire survivors.

# TABLE OF CONTENTS

# INTRODUCTION

**F**irst and foremost, we want you to know that it takes courage, bravery, and willingness to be vulnerable to begin your healing journey.

Experiencing trauma, of any kind, is hard. The toll that trauma can take on your mind, your body, and your spirit can make it difficult for you to move forward in life. Trauma can keep you mired in the moment of the traumatic experience, and over time, it can feel harder and harder to navigate through it. This can create anxiety, depression, hopelessness, fear, feelings of being stuck, and other symptoms of unprocessed trauma.

According to The National Council for Behavioral Health (2013), an estimated 70% of adults in the United States have experienced a traumatic event to some degree at least once in their lives. This means that roughly 223.4 million people have had to live with and process trauma. As reported by the American Psychiatric Association (2020), approximately one in eleven people will be diagnosed with posttraumatic stress disorder (PTSD) in their lifetime.

Trauma and the resulting disorder of PTSD can occur within a spectrum of experiences. One person's experience is no more or no less important than another person's experience. Though experiences may look different, the result is the same; pain, wounding, struggle, hopelessness, fear, and an inability to see light at the end of the tunnel are common for those who have experienced trauma. Whether it is an accident, assault, adverse childhood experience, mass shooting, emotional trauma, or natural disasters such as wildfires, earthquakes, or floods, the symptoms and feelings surrounding the experience are equally valid and common across the board.

*Sifting through the Ashes* will take you through the full spectrum of symptoms that are common to traumatic experiences and posttraumatic stress disorder. In this book, you read firsthand stories from survivors of the 2018 Camp Fire and about how their experiences have left a lasting imprint on them as they continue to heal. You will also learn about each of the symptoms associated with trauma and PTSD and how clinicians help clients process through and overcome these symptoms. We have included a special section, the "Clinician's Corner," in each chapter that provides education and insights into the clinical counselor's perspective and what we must consider when working with survivors of trauma.

In the Appendix, we provide a resource section where you can find important information, phone numbers or websites, and checklists to use to help you get the help you need. We also provide you with a resources page where you can find numerous self-assessments, daily practices, and interventions you can do yourself, in the comfort of your own space, to help you work through your feelings of anxiety, depression, or being stuck. You can find these interventions, practices, and assessments at the following site:
www.SiftingThroughTheAshesResources.com

You can use this book in conjunction with any current therapy or counseling. It can also be used for those not yet in counseling as a steppingstone toward your healing journey. *Sifting through the Ashes* can be a catalyst for you to make the brave decision to invest in yourself and seek help.

Included in this book is a special section dedicated to the stories and insights of the emergency personnel who courageously helped total strangers to safety. Survival was the number one priority, and the stories and related insights will give you a glimpse into the perspectives of those who made sure others got out first.

## Who is this book for?

*Sifting through the Ashes* is for anyone who struggles with their own trauma and desires more understanding about what they may be feeling and experiencing. We hope the information in this book will help to validate and normalize what may feel so isolating.

This book was also written for the loved ones of those affected by trauma who seek more education and understanding of what their friend, spouse, or family member may be experiencing. The tips and tools we have provided will better prepare you for handling whatever thoughts and feelings may come up for your loved one.

*Sifting through the Ashes* is for those who watched or lived the horror of any disaster or crisis through news channels and want to gain a better understanding of what survivors experienced, the totality of their loss and trauma, and how they overcame the tragedy. Please allow your compassion to open your heart to what others had to go through.

*Sifting through the Ashes* is for all the survivors who lived through the experience of the Camp Fire and continue to struggle with their memories and feelings. This book is intended to help you find some semblance of closure and resolve as you read your own stories and the stories of your neighbors and friends. You are not alone in your trauma. Sharing stories can bring a sense of community back to what was once a close-knit and humble town.

Be aware that some of the material in this book is sensitive in nature and has the possibility of activating thoughts and feelings about your own experiences with trauma. We encourage you to take breaks while reading, explore your feelings with a therapist or loved one, and keep a journal where you can write down anything that may come up for you while you read this book. The work depicts actual events in the lives of the survivors. While all persons within are actual individuals, names and identifying characteristics have been changed to respect their privacy. Permission was obtained by each individual whose story was told.

> **"Although the world is full of suffering, it is also full of the overcoming of it."**
> **–HELEN KELLER**

# PART 1:
# The Survivors' Stories

# ADAM'S STORY
## Ministry, Military, Medic

I woke up at 5:15 a.m. I was a coach at the gym and was to open the doors for a class that began at 5:30 a.m. We had about eighty members at the gym at that time. There were about seven to ten members that morning of November 8, 2018. One of them was the fire battalion chief. He was one of the main people who staged the firefighters.

After class was over, it was normal for me to go back home since I do personal training at home. I went back to my house and my wife went to work. She worked in Paradise at a dental office. About an hour later, around 7:30 a.m., I got a phone call from a friend who asked if I was evacuating. At that time, it was early, and I asked, "Why?"

"Don't you know there's a fire?" he asked.

I said, "No."

I thought he was nuts. I walked outside and I could see the smoke, but it looked far away. I didn't think it would reach Paradise. Plus, I didn't hear anything. The news wasn't saying anything. I didn't get any alerts.

Maybe a half hour later, my wife called and said, "Hey, listen, they are evacuating the schools and it might be something serious."

Living in Paradise, we have been evacuated several times. So, I said, "OK." I took her seriously, and I packed up some things. I am a very organized person. The funny thing is, I remember at this time, I said, "We need files." We had file boxes, but I was looking for other boxes and re-organizing the boxes with the files. I was putting things into the boxes and not going on with any urgency. Now, I could kick myself. Why wasn't I urgent about this? I don't know.

About fifteen minutes later, my wife got home. I had a few things by the door, and I said, "Why don't you grab our indoor cat and the dog, and I will keep loading things up." No urgency still. I thought we were good. At the same time, I was calling our CrossFit 8:30 a.m. class to cancel. As it turned out, people got back to me to let me know I saved their lives with that call. For some, the fire was in their backyards when they got my call.

I don't get over-excitable, and I love my wife, but she tends to carry that weight. I need to be the calm. I started a little laundry since I had all my workout clothes and none of them were clean. Again, no urgency. I got a call from a friend who couldn't get ahold of her husband asking if I could wake him up. They lived about a half mile away, so I jumped in my car and told my wife to keep packing her car and I would be right back. I drove a tenth of a mile and traffic was backed up. That's when it hit me. This was serious. I knew I would have to go it on foot. I called a firefighter friend and asked if someone could go wake up my friend's husband, and I went back home.

I told my wife to pack whatever she had into the car, take the dog and the cat, and go. I was pulling flammable things away from the house. We couldn't find the indoor/outdoor cat.

I promised my wife I wouldn't stay too long. This was where it got tough. I called my twelve-year-old daughter and told her I had all of her artwork in the house, but I couldn't take everything with me. I asked her what her favorite piece of artwork was, and I took pieces that I loved. I wanted to make sure I grabbed her stuff, too. She named a few things, and I said I would grab some of my favorites and her mom's favorites. I couldn't take everything. I have a little Toyota Yaris. I went to load my washer and dryer and my power went out. I didn't want to break my washer, thinking I didn't want to come home to a broken washer.

I took a lap around my house, calling the cat, hoping the cat would come back. I sprayed my house down with water and pulled the propane tanks away from the barbecue, trying to create a safe spot. I remember going into the house for a few seconds to look for the cat; I still thought I had time. I walked outside and the sky went black—totally black. It went from day to night.

Huge ashes and flames were falling from the sky. It was Armageddon, instantly. Within three minutes, I was still spraying the house down and calling the cat. I had maybe five minutes, tops. A fire truck pulled down my road and the firefighter asked what I was doing there. I told him I was looking for my cat. He said, "Listen, I will go to the end of your road, and if I come back out and you are not gone, I'm kicking you out of here."

He drove down the street and turned back, and I got into my car. That's when my heart broke. My daughter is a cat lover, and I couldn't find the cat. I realized I didn't even have time to go pee. I couldn't save the cat. I felt like I had disappointed my daughter and my wife. The cat is their pet.

As I left, the fire erupted and all I saw was a wall of flames coming toward me. It was a good five hundred yards away, creeping toward me. Across the street there was already a fire. I turned right on Pentz Road and was met by bumper-to-bumper traffic. The cars were crawling at a snail's pace. I could just see that wall of flames and barely stayed in front of it.

It took me almost five hours to get to my mom's place in Chico. The entire drive I was calling friends and asking if they were OK. I called my wife and my daughter and told them I couldn't find the cat. That was when I broke down. I couldn't find their fur baby. At the time, we didn't know our house was going to go up. I knew, even though I put water on my house, it wasn't going to be good. We lost our house.

I lived in Paradise since 1979, when I was two years old. I attended Ponderosa Elementary School and Paradise Intermediate and High Schools. I played T-ball, soccer, and was on the swim team. I played basketball, football, and soccer for the high school and was in Boy Scouts. I sang in the choir and was in the Drama Club. I was all over the place. Growing up, I had a few jobs in town. I worked as a lifeguard at the Paradise pool. My first job, at thirteen years old, was as a stock boy at the market on the corner of Stearns and Pentz Roads. It was called "Country Market" back then.

After high school graduation, I went to Los Angeles and later finished college in Redding at Simpson University. I wanted to be a pastor and got a seminary degree. I went through a difficult divorce about nine years into my ministry, switched gears, and went into the Air Force. I was in the Air Force for six years as a medic.

I came back to Paradise after being a medic. I wanted to be home again. I loved Paradise. I loved all of it. I loved being in the ministry and serving people. I loved serving in the military. When I returned to Paradise I worked in the emergency room for a while as a medic, but I didn't like the healthcare system in the civilian world. It was really abused.

I pulled out of that and transitioned into work as a personal fitness trainer. I worked my way into group training and became the director of group training and then transitioned into CrossFit. I was coaching and I was doing Odyssey, which is leadership coaching. I did some life coaching. I am not really a medic or a teacher, but I did do some substitute teaching when I came back with the district in Paradise.

We were able to go back to the property to see if our cat showed up. We got a phone call after the fire, around Christmas, saying our cat was found. Best Christmas present ever! My daughter was elated to see a picture of her cat, Lucy.

Because of the fire, I transitioned with my background in ministry, military, and medic, and I created a nonprofit in Paradise called "Paradise Stronger." It is a wellness center in Paradise, and it touches on not just fitness, but wellness education, nutrition, recovery, and counseling.

# Adam's Reflections

### What was the worst part of the experience for you that day?

I am a connector. I like that people are safe and that people feel like they belong to the community. I want people to feel that they know where to go. I remember I went to my mom's house that day. I was inviting everyone to my mom's house because I wanted everyone to be safe and know they had a place to go. The worst part was watching my community get torn apart. I knew my wife was safe. I knew no matter what, I would find a way out. But not knowing my community was going to be all right was heartbreaking.

### If you could have done anything differently, what would you have done?

I don't see myself as a hero, but I would have wanted to find people in Paradise and help them out.

### What have you learned from going through this experience?

A couple of things. My wife and I have always told each other all we need is each other. We lost 95% of our stuff and literally had the community taken apart. Knowing my wife was safe, and my daughter was safe, that's all I needed. I didn't need anything else.

As I was escaping the fire, I remember one of the things along that drive that stuck out to me was a car in front of me. It was a Jeep, and it had a tire cover that said, "Life is Good." Reminding me that I am OK. Life is good and I can handle this.

### Where do you feel that you are still struggling or stuck?

I want my wife to be happy. Learning the motto, we said to each other, "All we need is each other." Having that tested, it rang true. It is not just something to say. We lived it. I don't want my wife to live in fear.

### What keeps you going?

My wife. She is a helper. She is amazing. I have to force her to help herself. She is so independent. But deep down, she is still scared and needs someone around. We both do. Making sure I provide the life that I told myself and I told her dad I would provide for her.

### If you could give another survivor any advice, what would you say?

I want my community to be healthy and strong. Make something a priority and stick with that priority.

# Clinician's Corner
# Disaster Preparedness and
# Self-Talk

**A**dam positioned himself as the calm presence that his family needed at the time of the fire. This skill, which he learned in the military as a combat medic, became a pivotal point in his and his family's survival. When people go into panic, their fight-flight-freeze brain function kicks into hyperdrive, and any logic and reason tend to get pushed to the side. This is where many people do not think to grab certain items or important documents. This is because the brain is in straight survival mode.

Most of us are not trained in the military to be calm in times of crisis. Many people are skilled in this responsiveness because of their careers or life experience, but unless you have military experience, work in a hospital emergency room, or have any other crisis-oriented career, you may not know how to keep yourself in a calm and collected state.

Here are some important steps you can take to help you feel and be more prepared if you are ever caught in a situation where you have to think on your feet and possibly evacuate. With this preparedness also comes the added benefit of confidence in knowing that you are more prepared and ready if the time comes. We've included an extensive Disaster Assistance and

Preparedness Checklist inside this book as well as on the resources page here:
www.SiftingThroughTheAshesResources.com

# Disaster Assistance and Preparedness Checklist

| Mark "Yes" or "No" to All That Apply | YES | NO |
|---|---|---|
| 1. Pictures of the outside and inside of the house and property so you know what to document in case of an emergency | | |
| 2. Inventory of valuable household items | | |
| 3. Photocopies of important documents such as bank account numbers, identification cards, passports, credit cards, insurance policies, deeds, wills, stocks and bonds | | |
| 4. Important documents like social security cards, birth certificates, death certificates, and wedding certificates stored in a waterproof container | | |
| 5. Prescription medication | | |
| 6. Nonprescription medication such as vitamins and pain relievers | | |
| 7. Cash | | |
| 8. Extra phone, computer, and chargers for your electronic devices | | |
| 9. Water | | |
| 10. Three-day supply of nonperishable food such as meats, fruits and vegetables, nuts, canned juices, beans, comfort/snack foods, etc. | | |

| | | |
|---|---|---|
| 11. Manual can opener | | |
| 12. Paper cups, plates, and utensils | | |
| 13. Napkins and paper towels | | |
| 14. Tool kit | | |
| 15. First aid kit | | |
| 16. Whistle to signal for help | | |
| 17. Signal flare | | |
| 18. Fire extinguisher | | |
| 19. Batteries | | |
| 20. Battery-powered radio | | |
| 21. Matches and/or lighter | | |
| 22. Flashlights, candles, and lanterns | | |
| 23. Moist towelettes, toilet paper, soap, liquid detergent | | |
| 24. Personal hygiene items and feminine supplies | | |
| 25. Eyeglasses, contact lenses, and contact solution | | |
| 26. Hearing aids and batteries | | |
| 27. Clothing such as jacket or coat, long pants, long-sleeve shirts, sturdy shoes, hat and gloves, rain gear, etc. | | |
| 28. Warm blankets | | |
| 29. Bedding such as pillows and sheets | | |

| | | |
|---|---|---|
| 30. Pet supplies including food and extra water, important pet documents | | |
| 31. Disinfectant | | |
| 32. Chlorine bleach | | |
| 33. Waterproof bag | | |
| 34. Duct tape | | |
| 35. Mask or cotton T-shirt to filter the air | | |
| 36. Self-defense weapons such as pepper spray, etc. | | |
| 37. Games and other activities for children | | |
| 38. Paper, pens, and pencils | | |
| 39. Infant items such as diapers, formula, and bottles | | |
| 40. Full tank of gas | | |

You can also order free preparedness materials through the Federal Emergency Management Agency (FEMA), which can be shipped directly to you at no cost (ready.gov, 2021). Please see the Appendix for a list of disaster relief resources.

It is important to note that each situation is different, and your personal and family needs will be different. Take these recommendations as general guidelines that you may alter, tweak, or delete for your personal circumstances. If you do all the work now, you can prepare yourself in case of an emergency and keep you and your family safe.

One strong suggestion is to make photocopies or keep the originals of all important documents in one location, in a clearly labeled folder, so they can be easily retrieved if you need to evacuate immediately. These items should include birth certificates, social security cards, wedding licenses, insurance forms or claim paperwork, and all documents pertaining to your home and/or your finances. You could also create an inventory of your personal belongings and their estimated value, which would be helpful when dealing with insurance companies. We also suggest, if possible, that you have a backup credit card in this same place to use for emergency shelter, food, and medical needs.

As we write this section of the book, we are asking ourselves, what would we grab if we had to evacuate? Photos? Laptops with all our important information on them? Family heirlooms? Clothes? Make a list of all the items you and your family need to save, so, if the time comes, you can think clearly and be levelheaded about what is essential. In this digital age, it is easy to scan or upload photos onto flash drives or cloud services. We highly recommend scanning family photos into an electronic device, such as an optical disc or flash drive, and keeping that with your important documents.

Another suggestion is having a bin or box with all the items you may need if you are displaced for a couple of days. These might include a change of clothing, toiletries, pet food and water, a backup of medication, phone and laptop chargers, and nonperishable food or snacks. You might keep the document folder mentioned above in this bin as well. This bin or box could be kept in your car or anyplace else that would be easily accessible if you needed to flee.

The most important aspect of being prepared for an emergency is having an evacuation plan and meeting location for friends and family, a place where you would agree to meet if anything happened. This could be a restaurant, a hotel, a friend's house, or any other prearranged spot where you can reunite and reset.

Another aspect of Adam's story is the importance of self-talk, also called affirmations, mantras, mottos, or simple phrases you can say to yourself to keep yourself calm, rational, and moving forward. A Self-Talk Affirmations Checklist can be found on the resources page here: www.SiftingThroughTheAshesResources.com

Think of your brain like a computer. The thoughts we have are like programs for our mind that influence how we feel, how we react, and how we respond. Positive or forward momentum thoughts can help us stay in a mindset of moving forward. Positive self-talk seeks to bring the positive out of the negative to help you do better, go further, or just keep moving forward. This practice of positive self-talk is often the process that allows you to discover the obscured optimism, hope, and joy in any given situation (Jantz, 2016). As Adam shared in his reflections, he and his wife share the motto, "All we need is each other." This helped him move from survivor to thriver. Having this programming phase helped Adam perceive his situation as something that could be healed because he, his wife, and his daughter (and cat) were together and safe, and that was all that mattered.

Using self-talk and repeating mantras or affirmations can also help to reaffirm positive or neutral thoughts, especially when you have a negative inner dialogue with yourself. Your words and thoughts are like computer "programs," and your mind picks up and uses these "programs" as your perception of the world around you. Repeating a phrase that you might not totally believe will help you start to believe it. It's a "fake-it-until-you-make-it" program and can help you learn to stay calm, be positive, and move from victim to survivor to thriver. You can find a Victim-Survivor-Thriver Checklist on the resources page here: www.SiftingThroughTheAshesResources.com

# BONNIE'S STORY
## No Words

I feel so overwhelmed with grief. I just feel like this last fire took everything. I am really, really discouraged.

My nephew committed suicide in 2005, and I feel like I am in that same place. I had never believed in antidepressants, but it feels like a thirteen-year-old battle, and I worry about myself.

I've never been like this bad. My mom died. I also had a niece who committed suicide, then my dog died. It's loss after loss—then the fire. I start crying all the time. Every day it feels like just getting through the day.

I have to get a job. I have all these things to do, and it feels like I am juggling all the balls, it's just one more thing. Now I am living with my dad, and my son moved back to Paradise in March 2020. I can tell when he is not doing well because I don't hear from him, and he disconnects.

I feel damaged. Why does it have to be so hard? I have a problem going back up to Paradise. It took me over two years to drive up there. I don't have a desire to go back to Paradise. I feel like I'm putting my head in the sand. There's so much pressure and people are putting pressure on me to go up there and it pisses me off.

My friends say I just need a tour guide. I don't have to go if I don't want to. My dad is saying, "Oh, look at these pictures, you can go up there. There are a lot of people who left the state who are now returning to Paradise."

**This survivor is still so traumatized she can't even tell her story.**

# Clinician's Corner
# Depression and Suicidality

**B**onnie's circumstances are common, and we want to normalize feelings of depression and feeling as if you can't move on from your trauma. We all experience things in different ways, and there is no right or wrong way to process and heal. This section can bring some clarity, normalization, and hope if you are struggling with hopelessness, depression, and suicidality.

*Be aware that this section will talk about material that may be sensitive to some readers. The material is important, but you have the option to skip this section if you are not ready to read it.*

If you or someone you know is struggling with thoughts or feelings of wanting to hurt themself or planning to attempt suicide, please reach out to a mental health professional, or call the **National Suicide Prevention Lifeline** at **1-800-273-8255** or by dialing **988** on your phone. You can also connect to the **Crisis Text Line** by texting **HOME** to **741741** for free 24/7 crisis support. You can find additional Suicide and Crisis/ Disaster resources in the Appendix.

If you feel that you need to skip this section, please do so now.

A main theme that is apparent is the feeling of hopelessness that Bonnie expresses in what she can share of her story. She has had numerous losses, and the fire added to the deep grief she already felt. Hopelessness can occur when a person cannot see life in any other light than the darkness they have been in. Hopelessness can lead to depression, which can be understood as a system of beliefs, behaviors, and ways of relating to others that can keep you trapped (Leahy, 2021).

Depression can feel like you are in a dark hole of despair and has a number of signs and symptoms, some or all of which may be present. A clinical diagnosis of depression, or major depressive disorder, requires symptoms to be present for more than two weeks, while dysthymia, or persistent depressive disorder, requires symptomatic episodes to be present two years or more (National Institute of Mental Health-NIMH). Signs and symptoms of depression, according to NIMH, include, but are not limited to, the following:

- Persistent anxiousness, sadness, or a feeling of "emptiness"

- Hopelessness or pessimism

- Easily irritable

- Feelings of guilt, worthlessness, or helplessness

- No longer interested in pleasurable activities and hobbies

- Fatigue or a decrease in energy

- Restless feelings or having trouble staying still

- Having concentration difficulties

- Changes in appetite or unplanned weight changes

- Disruptions in sleep patterns which can include sleeping too little or sleeping too much

- Suicidality, which includes thoughts, feelings, and attempts to commit suicide

- Physical aches and pains, headaches, and even digestive issues with no known or clear cause

It should be made clear that not everyone will experience all of these symptoms, and they can be experienced differently by each person. If you or someone you know is experiencing any of these symptoms, the best encouragement we can offer is to get help from a mental health professional. You are not alone and, though you may not see a light at the end of the tunnel, talking to a therapist can be highly beneficial in helping you find a path back into the light. There are a few exercises to help you learn more about what you are feeling, and perhaps, to help make coping a little easier. Please take these exercises as they resonate with you and leave them if they do not.

A great way to monitor your feelings is to keep a journal or a log and "scale" how you are feeling every waking hour of the week (Leahy, 2021). We recommend starting with three to five times a day. Let's use the feeling of hopelessness, for example. On a scale of 0 to 10, with 0 meaning not at all hopeless (hopeful) and 10 meaning completely hopeless, track where your hopelessness lands. For this example, track in the morning, at midday, and at night before bed. Perhaps you are a scale of 4 in the morning, a scale of 6 at midday, and a scale of 9 at night. It is important to understand your moods throughout the day. If you start to see a pattern, it will be productive to plan more support during the times you need it the most. If you start to see a pattern of feeling more hopeless at night before bed, then you and your therapist can develop a strategic plan to provide you with additional support systems in the evening.

Another great exercise is to use an Enjoyable Activities Checklist to provide you with ideas and steps to find small joyous moments during your day. You can

find a Depression Symptom Checklist and the Enjoyable Activities Checklist on the resources page here:
www.SiftingThroughTheAshesResources.com

The Enjoyable Activities Checklist includes a number of activities to inspire small pleasures to help relieve feelings of despair. Some of the activities may include action items such as petting your dog or cat, smelling flowers, going for a walk, listening to music, or talking to a friend or family member. Many people find these activities helpful in relieving their feelings of hopelessness, if only for a minute. Another helpful exercise is mindfulness. Mindfulness is the practice of being in the here and now, in the present moment. Being present in the here and now allows the mind to focus on a specific thought that is not rooted in the past or reaching for the future. It is focused only on this very moment. It is impossible for your mind to think about more than one thing at a time, so focusing on one specific thing can help alleviate the pain of your current thoughts.

One easy practice is to slowly peel an orange or any other fragrant fruit and to focus on the smell of the fruit. As you peel the orange, close your eyes, take slow, deep breaths, and inhale the citrus aroma. What does the aroma remind you of? How does the aroma make you feel? Is it a strong or faint aroma?

Now, place a piece of orange in your mouth and focus on the taste and the texture. What does it taste like? Is it sweet or sour? Does the taste bring up any thoughts or memories? What does the texture feel like? Is it soft or firm? As you work your way through these questions, notice how you are feeling. If you are focused on the orange, you may feel a small sense of reprieve in your hopelessness, if even for a second. Notice how fast your thoughts revert back to the hopeless thoughts that are most likely automatic for you. Notice how your feelings may change once you become aware of your hopeless thoughts. Little practices like these, however simple and small, can have a large impact on how you feel over time and can contribute to the bolstering of your resilience. You can find other mindfulness activities on the resources page as well:

www.SiftingThroughTheAshesResources.com

Psychoeducation about suicidality is important to know and understand. Suicidality can be considered the thoughts, feelings, and actions toward ending one's own life (mentalhealth.gov, 2021). According to the Center for Disease Control and Prevention (CDC, 2021), suicide is a leading cause of death in the United States. In 2020, 45,979 people died by suicide. That is one death every eleven minutes. In 2020, 1.2 million people attempted suicide, 3.2 million people made a plan for suicide, and roughly 12.2 million people thought about suicide (CDC, 2021). We share these statistics because we want you to know that if you are struggling with thoughts and feelings of wanting to end your life, you are not alone. Mental health professionals are trained and have the experience to help you overcome your suicidality.

We've included a Suicide Risk, Protective, and Ideation Factors Checklist and Crisis Safety Plan in this section as well as on the resources page here:

www.SiftingThroughTheAshesResources.com

**National Suicide Prevention Lifeline at 1-800-273-8255**

# Suicide Risk, Protective, and Ideation Factors Checklist

| Risk Factors:<br><br>Mark "Yes" or "No" to All That Apply | YES | NO |
| --- | --- | --- |
| 1. I have had a past suicide attempt (at least once) | | |
| 2. I have been diagnosed with a mental illness (major depressive, bipolar, anxiety, schizophrenia, etc.) | | |
| 3. I have a history of suicide in my family | | |
| 4. I have chronic illness and/or pain | | |
| 5. I am unemployed | | |
| 6. I have experienced childhood abuse and neglect | | |
| 7. I am a military veteran | | |
| 8. I am a first responder | | |
| 9. I have access to guns | | |
| 10. I have limited access to mental healthcare | | |

| Protective Factors:<br><br>Mark "Yes" or "No" to All That Apply | YES | NO |
|---|---|---|
| 1. I have a positive outlook on life, overall | | |
| 2. I am able to accept things as they are | | |
| 3. I have children at home | | |
| 4. I am part of a religious group | | |
| 5. I am close to my family | | |
| 6. I have strong support from friends | | |
| 7. I actively seek mental health support when I need it | | |
| 8. I feel cared for and loved | | |
| 9. I am currently employed | | |
| 10. I have a sense of control over my life | | |

| **Suicidal Ideation Factors:**<br><br>Mark "Yes" or "No" to All That Currently Apply | YES | NO |
|---|---|---|
| 1. I have persistent thoughts of suicide | | |
| 2. I have thought about and have a method of how I would attempt suicide | | |
| 3. I have begun to work out the details of how I would attempt suicide | | |
| 4. I intend to carry out my plan | | |
| 5. I acknowledge I am at risk of harming myself and I will actively seek help | | |

# Crisis Safety Plan

**What are some warning signs that can determine if I may be in a crisis?**

    1. _____

    2. _____

    3. _____


**What are some coping strategies I can use to prevent a crisis?**

    1. _____

    2. _____

    3. _____


**What are the items I need to remove in my environment to prevent myself from harm?**

    1. _____

    2. _____

    3. _____

    4. _____

## Who are the people whom I can ask for help?

1. Name: _____ Phone: _____

2. Name: _____ Phone: _____

3. Name: _____ Phone: _____


## Who are the professional mental health clinicians and agencies I can contact during a crisis?

1. Agency/Clinician: _____ Phone: _____

2. Agency/Clinician: _____ Phone: _____


## The one thing that is most important to me and worth living for is:

_____

# CASEY'S STORY
## Moving Forward

**I** was home as I didn't start work until nine in the morning. I could see the plumes of smoke in the distance. I felt OK. It was just another wildfire. Growing up in Susanville, we were used to wildfires. More than ten years ago, when I was in middle school, there was the "Devil's Fire" in Susanville. It came within a half or a quarter mile of my middle school. It was just another massive wildfire. Some parts of the town were under evacuations. There was ash. I knew it was pretty bad. When you grow up in the mountains, it is a typical thing during the summertime. For me, November 8, 2018 felt like just another day. I didn't feel like there was any danger, but my wife was uneasy about it.

My wife and I work at the same company, and she went to work at 8 a.m. As I was drinking coffee and watching the news, she was freaking out. She called me three times, yelling at me. She told me to get ready. I told her I was fine and not to worry about it. We had been through this—it wasn't a big deal.

My wife felt something was off. She sent me some pictures. The fire was getting closer, but I still didn't think it was going to be bad. I think it was about 9:15 a.m. when I started taking pictures off the walls, but I wasn't panicked. Maybe a half hour later, it went from daylight to nighttime. Then I thought, OK, something was a little off. That's not normal. So, I started working a little faster to get everything. A little uneasiness set in. I still wasn't worried about anything. At the same time, my wife was hearing the officers going up and down the main streets. They were using the loudspeakers, saying we needed to get out—time to evacuate. I never heard anything. There was nothing on the news. I searched the news and the only thing there was a fire in Pulga. That's all it was. I wasn't worried about it as there were no news alerts telling us to get out.

I gathered everything I could to the best of my knowledge. I grabbed the cat's ashes and my wife's jewelry. I still had hope that we wouldn't lose the apartment, so I grabbed a weekend's worth of clothes for both of us. I ended up losing 90% of my clothing because of this. I left a few things behind since I didn't think about grabbing them, I guess. Now it seems pretty dumb, but there was a fire going. The major thing I left behind was my dog tags from the military. Those were the ones I wore in Iraq. That just sucks. I joined the National Guard in 2005. I guess that helped with the fire situation. Because of my military experience, I was able to stay calm.

I grabbed the expensive TV because my wife said I still owed money on it. I grabbed photos of my mom when she was younger. I am thankful I grabbed those photos that were from my grandmother. I grabbed some of my military stuff. My wife was home by then so we put everything we could in the vehicles. That took about twenty-five minutes. We got what we thought we need-ed—all of our personal documents and all my military paperwork as well as anything that was sentimental to us.

I could hear propane tanks exploding. I noticed fifty yards behind the apartment there was a fire, and

I could see the flames. We had to go. My wife said my military voice came out. I was told I yelled at her to get in her car and go. Habit kicked in, and I locked the front door, and I am not sure why.

After that, we both looked at the apartment for half a second and hoped it would survive. We both weren't sure. We got into our vehicles and left the complex. Someone let us into the line of vehicles on the road. We sat on Elliott Road for forty-five minutes. I made sure my wife was in front of me the whole time. I knew the smoke was bad, so I gave her my bandanna that I kept in the car. It helped as a filter, and I used my shirt.

She was in front of me the whole time, as we both went the same direction to get out of Paradise. People were freaking out. It's just human nature. My wife did very well. She kept calm. She didn't drive erratically. I stayed with her all the way down to Pearson Road. It merged a quarter mile from Skyway. My wife merged and ten to twelve cars just pushed their way in. I finally got in. By the time I merged, my wife was merging onto Skyway.

We were on the phone off and on, because she was also on the phone with her mother. I just stayed on the line. I tried keeping her calm. I told her everything was OK to the best of my ability. Words are only words, but mentally I was trying to keep her calm. When my wife was on Skyway, she got through with the fire on both sides. She called me as I was hitting that section. I was driving, and another driver freaked out and slammed on their brakes. It was understandable. It was hard to see since we were going through black smoke. I hit my brakes, and thankfully the car behind me didn't rear-end me. I went past them and broke through the smoke and saw blue skies on the northbound side of Skyway.

I was trying to catch up with my wife. Halfway down, I ended up catching up with her at Bruce Road at the end of Skyway in Chico. I followed her all the way down to Kmart. I got out, and she met up with her coworkers. They cried it out and exchanged hugs. I went to use the bathroom at Kmart and then called my parents to tell them we were safe. They were not happy since I didn't call them before, but my mind was not focused on calling them. My mind was focused on getting my wife of three weeks out safely.

After a few hours, my wife went straight to work in Red Bluff. I drove to Corning and met up with my wife that night. The next morning, we both went to work and didn't stop working for the next few months until we moved to Montana. Working helped us keep our minds off of everything. The job we did was trying to keep our clients safe and give them a sense of normalcy. We would also help move everything from hotel room to hotel room and make sure everyone got situated.

At one point, I stepped in and did my wife's job. It was not something I enjoyed. My patience was thin. We went from a hotel room the first night to staying with my wife's friend from high school to getting an apartment in Oroville. Our apartment was not in the greatest part of Oroville. We didn't feel safe. Three of the power line generators blew when we were there, and we ended up with no electricity for a while.

That apartment was shady beyond reason. The front door could have been kicked in very easily. I had my pistol by my side every night. It was also pretty drafty, and we could smell the smoke. We spent most of our days in Red Bluff, driving fifty miles there and fifty miles back, carpooling with each other, and we did that for work until late December. We were helping out as much as we could. The last week we worked, we finally broke it to everyone that we had to go.

Work helped us, and we did what we had to do. A friend of ours cooked dinners for us. For the most part, it was all work—about sixteen hours a day. My wife's family is originally from Montana. I fell in love with the area and with the mountains and snow. We now live in Missoula, with mountains all around us. It's a gorgeous place, very outdoorsy. Life is better here. We got a house within a year of the Camp Fire. I got my truck. My wife got her Jeep. We are not victims; rather, we are survivors.

# Casey's Reflections

***Out of the whole experience, what was the worst experience for you?***

I would say losing something that I grew to love. We had only been in Paradise a few months, but we grew to love it very quickly. It was a lot better living than in Chico, and work was very close. The cost of living was less and it was a good, quality place to be. It was just an all-around great community. We felt safe and had no issues with anyone. It had a small-town feel and there were beautiful parks. It was better than Susanville. There was a lot less drama. I loved that the community would get together for Johnny Appleseed or Gold Nugget Days. We hung out with our coworkers.

***If you could have done anything differently that day, what would you have done?***

I guess I don't know. I got my wife out safely; that was my main goal. I guess I would have taken photos of everything for records. I guess I would have grabbed more sentimental things such as my dog tags, my wife's wedding dress, and some other things from her family. We grabbed most of the essentials. I think we left at a good time. She was ahead of me, and she could get out. I think we did pretty well. We had more time to get out than others. There is nothing I would change, I guess.

## What have you learned going through this experience?

I don't feel like it has really affected me. That seems kind of weird. I guess anger-wise, I snapped easier. I don't feel it emotionally. It doesn't affect me. I don't feel sadness or anything. Maybe it is my military training that allows me to compartmentalize everything and keep a level head. Whatever happens, happens. I try my hardest not to control anything. Go day by day.

## Are there any areas where you are still struggling or stuck?

I guess my motivation is lower. I slacked on my photography after the fire. I love photography. I just don't have the urge to do it now. I haven't found the time to do it. I don't have a passion anymore. The fire took that away.

## If you could give another survivor any advice, what would you say?

Don't let it define you. It is hard to get past it because the memory of that day is going to be there. The PTSD from that day will be there. All you can do is accept it, push through it, don't let it define you, and continue living your life to the best of your ability. Find another place to fall in love with or rebuild your life. Keep looking up and realize how quickly things can change but accept what it is. Learn to look to the future and go day by day. It is a massive experience. It is an experience that brings us all together as a community. Paradise will always be ours and always brings us to-gether. The tattoos on our wrists say, "It will always be home. Paradise is your heart home."

# Clinician's Corner
# Compartmentalization and
# Victim Mentality

Casey's response is somewhat unique since his military experience trained him to think and perform under pressure in order to get himself and his wife to safety. His training was crucial for him in that he was able to keep what looked like, on the outside, a cool and collected response to the emergency of the Camp Fire. As Casey stated, it is possible that he learned to compartmentalize his environment from his military experience.

Compartmentalization, as a trauma response, is a more controlled defense mechanism that suppresses thoughts and emotions so that logic and action can occur in order to complete a specific task or do a specific job. As in Casey's story, he essentially didn't have time to be emotional because he had to get himself and his wife to safety. Compartmentalization in other professions such as firefighters, first responders, emergency room staff, and of course, combat, can also be observed.

Compartmentalization, or disconnecting, has its advantages. As mentioned above, it allows a person to separate their emotional body from the reality of their physical experience so they can engage in a specific function or behavior. Without compartmentalization, emotion would take over and one may not be able to respond to the experience in an intentional and logical way. Sometimes, however, once the trauma or high-stress experience is no longer a threat, emotions that were suppressed bubble up in a way that is slightly different than if each emotion had been felt, processed, and dealt with.

Emotions may come up all at the same time and can often feel overwhelming to the person feeling them. Maybe you are sad, angry, grateful, and shocked all at the same time. This is completely normal and is common in the processing of trauma. After a trauma or traumatic event occurs, it often takes many months or even years for the emotions that were suppressed during the event to start showing themselves in a person's life. This is mainly due to compartmentalization. If you are experiencing an increase of thoughts and emotions from the Camp Fire, or if you are experiencing emotions starting to come up from any other traumatic event, be assured that it is absolutely all right, and it is completely normal.

One disadvantage of compartmentalization is that you can become emotionally unavailable to others (Insights, 2019). With compartmentalization, because your emotions are kept separate and suppressed from your lived reality, it is very possible that those who make up your lived reality (spouses, children, friends, family, etc.) will experience the emotional unavailability that compartmentalization creates.

It can be extremely difficult for loved ones to feel connected or have emotional intimacy with someone who compartmentalizes their emotions. They can feel distant, left out, misunderstood, and unloved. There are many more difficulties in loving someone who is emotionally distant. If you are the type of person who compartmentalizes, or if you feel emotionally unavailable, know that you are perfectly normal. It is a trauma response used as a coping mechanism to keep you safe.

Working with a therapist to reconnect to or become aware of your emotions and embark on the process of healing them can yield great benefit to not only you but your loved ones as well. It can seem scary to begin to feel negative emotions that have been suppressed for any amount of time, so it is important that you take your time, go slow, and speak to a professional who can work with you through the process.

Another important factor we would like to normalize for you is the idea of victim mentality. We want to make sure to talk about this concept because it is commonly used in social media, mainstream talk, and in most non-therapeutic settings. Victim mentality, or victim mindset, can be described as the personality trait of a person who feels that things that happen in their life are always the fault of someone or something else (Kaufman, 2020). When talking about trauma, using the terminology of "victim mentality" is a slippery slope because, most often in trauma, the victim is genuinely a victim of the act, behavior, or event. We want to validate your experience and any event or action against you in which you did not or do not have control, say, or authority over your life in any way.

The idea of victim mentality, while it may be used as a general term for anyone who perceives themself as a victim, can sometimes feel hurtful, invalidating, and minimizing. The feeling of victimhood comes from a wound, a pain, and most often stems from an early-childhood experience where a parent or caretaker did not help you to process the trauma or validate your experience, leaving your little-child self constantly in a state of survival. Each event or incident after that only solidified the core wounding throughout your life.

Working with a therapist to heal the original wounding, and to empower yourself to feel you have control over your life, can help you move away from victim to survivor and into thriver. Cognitive behavioral therapy (CBT) can be extremely useful for healing that wound and taking charge of your life. The basis for CBT is that how you think affects how you feel. How you feel then drives your actions and behaviors, which ultimately re-inforces your thoughts (Davis, 2018). You can see how this becomes a vicious cycle.

Most people do not know how to get off this mer-ry-go-round of negative thoughts. However, there are real-life solutions that can help you start to shift the "victim" mentality into one of empowerment. You can start by reframing your thoughts from negative thought forms into more positive or neutral thought forms. Get-ting into the practice of reframing your thoughts will rewrite the neural pathways in your brain that hold a specific thought. Like carving a new river into the side of the mountain, this process takes time. Your old thought has been traveling the same "river" for a substantial amount of time; rewriting it will take time, effort, and intention until it becomes automatic or second nature.

First, decide what you want changed in your life. Just pick one thing. Is it a better job? Or maybe to leave a relationship? Choose one aspect of your life you want to see improved or shifted.

Second, imagine how that improvement or shift would make you feel. Do you feel relieved? Or maybe supported, free, empowered? Decide what it would feel like to have that part of your life be different.

Now that you are visualizing the shift you want to see and you are connecting to the emotion that shift would generate, work on reframing your thoughts about it. For the third step, connect with the emotion you iden-tified with in step two. Sit with it for a few minutes and allow yourself to visualize and embody that emotion. It is completely OK if this is difficult to do. It can often be difficult to connect to an emotion you have never felt before or are not currently experiencing. This is why it takes practice.

Once you have fully connected with this new emotion, consider how a person who feels this way would think. What thoughts would you need to have in order to feel this new emotion? As an example, perhaps you want to find financial freedom. To experience financial freedom, what would make you feel relieved and at peace? Can you feel it? What thoughts would a person with peace and financial freedom think? One thought might be, "I am fully supported in life and abundance comes effortlessly to me." Another thought that provokes feelings of relief and peace is, "I can overcome any obstacle and have complete control over how I respond to life." This takes practice, intention, and effort.

We know you can overcome your negative thoughts. We all have them. You can shift from victim to survivor and into thriver. You can find our Cognitive Behavioral Therapy Techniques on the resources page here: www.SiftingThroughTheAshesResources.com

As we have learned from Casey's story, life events do not have to define you. You can choose to accept the events as part of your narrative, do the work to heal the wounds your trauma has caused, and move forward with a victor mindset. As Casey beautifully states, "Continue living your life to the best of your ability."

# AMY'S STORY
## That Guy

Our worries from Wednesday, November 7, 2018, were rapidly replaced in less than twenty-four hours. As three generations of our family loaded up what we could in twenty minutes, we scrambled to get out of town. We watched day turn to night on the morning of November 8 while we sat on Oliver Road for hours. Our daughter, son-in-law, four-year-old granddaughter, and two-month-old grandson were in the truck in front of us with the dogs. We followed with two of our three cats. The third ran off and was never found.

By the time we got through the intersection at Bille Road, the wind was howling and explosions went off every few seconds. Though terrifying, nobody panicked. We discussed everything matter-of-factly. We watched the tree branches whipping wildly, silently praying they wouldn't fall on us.

It was somewhere near Sunset and Castle Roads on Oliver where we encountered "that guy." He was careening across front yards in a large pickup truck with his son who was about eight or nine in the passenger seat. He was hauling a bass boat. I rolled down the window and asked what he was doing. He yelled, "I'm just getting out of the way so people can get by."

That was a lie. He quickly cut in front of our kid's truck. Many people got out of their cars asking what he was doing. I walked up and said, "You told us you were going to park and get out of the way."

"I lied," he said. He left his shaking son standing on the side of the road.

An old man, probably in his eighties, stood behind me, also wondering what was going on. "That guy" cussed and swore at us. I explained that my grandchildren were in the truck he cut off and one of them was just an infant. He screamed how he didn't care, and we should all just go home and burn. He was going to get his boat out. The old man tried to approach him, but he waved his arms angrily and told everyone to get away from him.

"Sue me, I'm an asshole," he said. The old man hugged me as we walked back to our cars in disbelief.

My daughter asked what was said and I told her I would tell her later. I didn't want to cause any more tension for any of us.

About an hour later, we were able to turn onto Skyway. It was fully ablaze, but we were grateful to be moving. We watched in awe as both sides of our main strip burned. Roofs were collapsing and flames engulfed the ponderosa pines like torches. By the time we got to the V at Skyway, traffic was being directed down both sides. The kids were directed to the right and we were directed left. In front of us, a man in an old Mercedes stopped as the sheriff waved his arms frantically for the man to move, but he was confused. He didn't want to drive the wrong way down Skyway. He looked as though he might not have driven that car in many years and probably only used it to escape. Finally, he proceeded and drove ahead slowly. We passed him. Fire trucks were coming toward us as we weaved through the confusion.

The wood from the guard rails burned and chunks of embers slammed into the bottom of the car. Cell phone service returned, and I called my mother on the East Coast who had no knowledge of the fire. I was preparing to say goodbye.

My younger daughter, an EMT who was living in the valley, signed up for a strike team. I called and begged her not to come into town.

Finally, the black sky turned blue once again. The kids and grandkids made it to safety in Chico. We were all going to be united again. Just after they arrived in Chico, a pickup truck blew up and started a new fire, closing parts of Highway 99. We were diverted and took a detour, finally meeting up with them at Sierra Nevada Brewing Company.

We smelled like smoke and looked like we went through a war. The wait staff didn't have a grasp quite yet of the situation and gave us strange and sideways looks. We had lunch and tried to decide what our next move would be. Our daughter told us that as they were driving down Skyway, they passed the guy with the boat. Apparently our four-year-old granddaughter gritted her teeth and squinted her eyes with a deep glare as she pointed to him and said, "Aaaaarrrrr, that guy."

# Clinician's Corner
# Selfishness in Others

**W**hen faced with a trauma or tragedy such as the Camp Fire, we wish we could say that every human being responds with kindness and compassion. We wish we could say that everyone works together for the sake of the whole, but we have all watched enough reality television to know there are always those one or two people who only think about themselves. It sounds like this was the type of person that Amy, her family, and countless others encountered on that day.

There are two ways that Amy, or any of us, can look at "that guy." First is that he is "that guy" who is selfish, rude, uncompassionate, and possibly even materialistic, saving his boat before human lives. Or second, he is "that guy" who is so wounded and disconnected from himself and others that, in the face of trauma and death and loss, self-survival is all he knows. One thing all of us, every human being, must remember is that the way other people treat us has absolutely nothing to do with us. It just doesn't, plain and simple. It does, however, have everything to do with how that other person feels about themself.

In truth, self-centeredness is actually a coping mechanism for trauma, abuse, and/or PTSD. A person who battles with trauma, abuse, or PTSD can live in such a haze of existence that it sometimes makes it hard or impossible to put the needs of others before your own (Rosenthal, 2013). With PTSD, there is so much focus on the inside that the outside, including the needs of other people, essentially is mute. This could explain the lack of compassion in some people during or after tragedies such as the Camp Fire. We don't know. We are not in the mind or the heart of "that guy." We can, however, say that with every "bad apple" of an experience we see countless other experiences of love, community, compassion, and triumph. Those are the stories we hold in our hearts and our minds.

If we can start seeing other people's negativity, selfishness, attitudes, and poor behaviors as coping mechanisms for something deeper, it is easier to prevent ourselves from taking on that same negativity. The man from Amy's story has a lifetime of experiences that shaped who he is and how he reacts to life, especially in chaos and emergencies like the Camp Fire. The man from the story is not just that one individual, he is all over, in every town, in every state, in every tragedy.

Reaction to any circumstance is from an unaware state of consciousness, whereas a response comes from a more aware and evolved state of consciousness where an individual acts and behaves from a place of healing and growth. In other words, a person reacts from subconscious "survival" and preservation of self. On the other hand, a person may respond from a conscious "good for all" and preservation of the whole.

This is also sometimes seen when individuals loot items, destroy property, or capitalize for financial gain on trauma, tragedy, chaos, and the vulnerability of the victims. Underneath these behaviors is an emotional entitlement which usually manifests from a trauma or victimization experience in the past. How that person views the world will determine what they do with the opportunity.

Negative mindsets and perspectives can sometimes lead someone to believe that the world owes them something. For whatever reason, the experience formed that individual's past and has left them feeling like they were not provided for, supported, paid what was due, or any other feeling of injustice. Therefore, their perspective takes on a "why should I do for others" energy, and it is evident in their attitude and behaviors. Again, we want to emphasize that this type of perspective or behavior is a coping mechanism. Even if it does not feel good being on the receiving end, that person is trying to cope the best they can with the level or lack of awareness and tools they have.

Having a positive mindset or neutral perspective of the world can produce much different outcomes than having a negative mindset. Those who see themselves as a part of the world rather than in battle with the world often see themselves as a part of the whole. This frequently results in a tendency to help, care about, and support other people. These types of people usually have a "how can I help" or "what is best for the majority" attitude, and this shows in their actions and behaviors. You can find a Kindness and Compassion Checklist on the resources page here:
www.SiftingThroughTheAshesResources.com

The moral of the story, especially Amy's story, is that there will be difficult or selfish people in all situations, circumstances, and events. The goal is to release grudges, negative perspectives, toxic relationships, and other vessels of negativity in your life. It may feel difficult at first, but once you have started to release your grip, letting go becomes increasingly easier (Scott, 2021). You can feel when you take on that negative energy from any experience with "that guy" or just a difficult person. We have all felt it. Our chest tightens, we get really angry, it's all we can think or talk about. It festers, and maybe we cannot sleep because we are just so bothered by it. This means that you have taken on that person's negative and unproductive mindset and energy. Give it back. It is not yours.

We recommend deep, diaphragmatic breathing paired with calming, guided meditative music. You can visualize yourself letting go of the annoyance, the anger, the festering. See it leaving your body and returning home to its rightful owner. To learn more about diaphragmatic breathing and relaxation techniques, visit the resources page here:

www.SiftingThroughTheAshesResources.com

# SHARON'S STORY
## Mass Exodus

It was 6:30 a.m. on November 8, 2018, when our grandchildren were dropped off at our house. It was a typical weekday. The kids nestled in and watched some cartoons before school was to start. An orange glow shone through the windows, which I thought seemed odd. My husband said it was probably just the sunrise. When I went to walk my granddaughter to school across the street, the sky was smoky and ash and embers filled the air.

I ran into a tow truck driver with his young daughter. He told me there was no school and we were being evacuated. I was shocked. I took the kids back to our home. There was a spot fire burning in the park and some men came to put it out. All of this came without any warning, no news, and no phone calls. Before we knew it, the sheriff's department came through the mobile home park telling us to "Leave now!"

We grabbed our pets and our medications. We grabbed all we could. My son drove one of our cars with his dog and cat. I drove our other car with my husband, grandchildren, and our dog. The scene was absolutely unreal. As we departed our driveway, we saw the empty lot on the corner was on fire. All the trees were burning.

My little granddaughter asked, "Grandma, are we going to be all right?" I didn't know if we would. We moved at a snail's pace on Wagstaff. Typically, you could drive the length of Paradise in mere minutes. The winds were higher than I'd ever seen in the twenty-six years we lived in the area. Embers were swirling all around us. It was daytime, but it was dark like midnight. People around us seemed to be holding it together as trees went up in flames on both sides of the road. Homes were burning down, and thick, black smoke blanketed us. It took hours to get from Wagstaff to Skyway. We heard explosion after explosion. I'm guessing it was propane tanks.

I talked on my cell phone to my sister, and I wondered if I would ever see her again. I talked to my brother-in-law, my pastor, and my other sons who were all anxious to know if we were in a safe place. All I could think was that I was on a mountain that was on fire. No, I didn't think I was in a safe place. Telephone poles and trees on fire were crashing down on the road. My dear little grandchildren were being so good. I worried about my son, who was driving in the other car. I couldn't see him, and I was hoping he was missing the trees and utility poles in the roadways. I had never been so fearful. I am grateful to God for getting us out of that inferno alive.

It took us six hours to get from our home to Chico, which is usually about a twenty-minute trip. Once in Chico, we stopped at a gas station to get gas and use the restroom. The restrooms were full so we headed to our son's place of work to get a key to his home. We stayed there that night. We were safe at last.

The City of Chico turned dark as smoke poured down from the mountains. It was hard to breathe. We coughed a lot. That night we learned the blaze was dubbed the "Camp Fire."

The next day we went to my sister-in-law's home in Corning. My son's family with the grandchildren went to a motel in Willows. They ended up moving from motel to motel to motel.

The repercussions of the fire proved to escalate over time. Yes, we were out of harm's way, but the emotional distress feels never-ending. Aside from the constant anxiety, there's the displacement. Red Bluff was the closest we could get to home. The greed and price gouging following the fire felt like an extra kick in the face.

Finally, sixteen months after the fire, we were able to move to Chico where my husband's doctors' appointments were. We moved to Chico on April 18, 2020. We were so excited to celebrate our thirty-second wedding anniversary in our new home on April 22, 2020. Five days after our anniversary, my husband died. This was my greatest loss. He was my everything.

It was more than just a fire, much more. The loss continues. It hasn't gotten easier. In fact, it's gotten more difficult to deal with and look back on, especially the loss of my husband. Don't get me wrong, I am very grateful to have my life and the lives of my family. But my son and his family lost their home in Magalia, along with their dog. My niece's home in Magalia is also gone. We lost friends, neighbors, and landmarks.

It might be rebuilt someday, but it will never be the same Paradise we all knew. It's too bad PG&E neglected to maintain its equipment for so long. People's lives were lost, eighty-five of them. Some didn't lose their lives in the fire but as a result of the fire. It's etched in our memories forever.

# Sharon's Reflections

### What was your worst part of your experience?

Driving out of the fire. Having my grandkids in the back seat. My husband trying to comfort me. To see all those fires. Everywhere you looked, there was a fire. It took six hours to get out of the area. Six hours of shock. At one point I called my sister and told her, "I'm not sure that I'll see you again." Worrying about how everyone was going to escape the fire. Shock of getting out. Genuine fear—never had fear like that before.

### Given the chance, what do you think you would do differently if you could?

I'd gather up more things. I was told by the fire department to go immediately, so I left many items behind I wish I still had. I would have grabbed our medications, clothing, personal things, and pictures.

### What keeps you going?

God. My relationship with God is what keeps me going.

### If you could give another survivor any advice, what would it be?

Don't give up. God's got a plan for you, too. It's rough, and we'll never forget the fire, but maybe it's a part of your story. It's bigger than any of us but it's not bigger than God. Give it all to God.

### Where do you still feel stuck?

I feel stuck in limbo waiting on settlements so that I can make permanent change for my life.

### What do you miss about Paradise?

The peace and quiet and the regularity. Paradise was home. I used to walk and bike up and down the road hills. It's so peaceful there. I had all my pictures. The serenity.

# Clinician's Corner
# Complicated Grief and Leaning into Faith

In Sharon's story, the loss of her home and the life she knew in Paradise was just the tip of the iceberg in her pain and sorrow, just as it might be for you, too. It was the loss of her husband after the fire that affected Sharon the most. As she states, her greatest loss was her husband. A loss of that magnitude only compounds and complicates the already traumatic experience of escaping and surviving the Camp Fire.

Sharon is experiencing what therapists call complicated grief, a grief so deep and complex that it can feel as though one can never recover from it. Most people will experience a "normal" period of grief and loss in which the typical feelings of bereavement are present but decrease over time (Mayo Clinic, 2021). Feelings of pain, sorrow, numbness, guilt, and even anger are expected. As the individual processes their loss, eventually these feelings and symptoms start to ease, and moving forward in life seems more manageable. In complicated grief, the feelings of loss are debilitating and do not improve over time. This is also known as Persistent Complex Bereavement Disorder, in which the intense feelings of bereavement last over one year (Mayo Clinic, 2021). You can find a Complicated Grief Symptom Checklist here: www.SiftingThroughTheAshesResources.com

As Sharon shares, it has been hard for her to look back on the experience. The pain and emotion that comes up for her is a reminder of the loss of her husband. In compounded loss, or losses that appear to build upon one another, it can be difficult for a person to process the emotions of the loss because there is so much of it. It is important to try to address the pain and emotions that come along with the complicated grief and compounded loss. It is normal to avoid the emotions, numbing them out with dissociation, substance use, apathy activities, or any other behavior or activity that keeps you from feeling the emotions.

A powerful intervention is to write a letter to your deceased loved one. It is common for there to be so much pain and emotion that it gets backed up in our emotional bodies because there is a resistance to feeling it. There are thoughts, words, memories, hopes, dreams, and feelings that are associated with the person we lost. Because our suffering comes from resisting those things, we tend to bottle them up. Writing a letter to your deceased loved one can help you express those thoughts and emotions and get them moving out of that emotional body and into a healing movement.

There is growth and healing in weeping. When you are moved to weep, you are moving emotions. It may not be joyful, but the space it creates in the healing journey is necessary for a new normal and lighter experience. In this letter, you can say everything you feel you need to say. If you need to be angry, then be angry. If you need to look back on fond memories, then do so. The goal is to get all those thoughts, words, memories, hopes, dreams, and feelings out of your head and heart and into the air for clearing.

Complex grief can also affect a person's mental, emotional, and physical well-being because the loss is so deep. Other symptoms that may manifest are depression, anxiety, PTSD, sleep disturbances, increased physical illness such as high blood pressure or heart disease, substance use/abuse, long-term difficulty with daily functioning, and suicidal thoughts and behaviors (Mayo Clinic, 2021). We encourage you to make an appointment with a medical professional if you believe your health has been influenced by a deep, complicated grief.

It is possible that people with complicated grief may consider suicide. If you or anyone you know is thinking about suicide, talk to someone you trust. If you think you or anyone you know may act on suicidal feelings, call 911 or your local emergency services number right away. Or call a suicide hotline number. **In the United States, call the National Suicide Prevention Lifeline at 1-800-273-TALK (1-800-273-8255) to reach a trained counselor or dial 988 for the Suicide Crisis Lifeline.**

In Sharon's story, she heavily leans into her faith and her relationship with God. Sharon experienced loss after loss, from losing her home and her sense of peace to losing her husband, but it is her connection to God that keeps her going. Faith can look different to each person. Each person has a unique perspective of God, universe, or higher power. The US Department of Veteran Affairs (2021) defines spirituality as an inner belief system providing an individual with meaning and purpose in life, a sense of sacredness of life, and a vision for the betterment of the world. In whatever way you believe or don't believe, you can make it work for you. Leaning into faith after trauma can have a healing impact on a person's life. In faith, there can be a comfort in feeling as though a power larger than the trauma is in control and, as Sharon stated, God has a plan. If you feel you need additional support in faith, spirituality, or religion, you are encouraged to seek out assistance from professionals in religion or faith to help you.

Faith can bring sources of support in the form of fellowships, worships, music, prayer, meditation, and other activities that provide comfort to help you through the pain of deep grief and loss. Finding purpose and meaning from the trauma, the loss, and the pain does not make the loss any less important or impactful to you. It can, however, be a catalyst for rewriting your life's story and how it will end. We cannot control what happens to us, big or small, but we can control how we respond to it. You are a thriver, and you can turn your tragedy into one of life's greatest underdog stories.

# JULIE'S STORY
# Memories Lost: The Fire Still Burns

That morning I was supposed to be at work at 11 a.m. By that time, the town was all but gone. It was also the last day I was supposed to work before I started a one-week vacation, a staycation so I could clean up my garage and get organized before the holidays.

Our youngest daughter was nine at the time, and she was sick and not in school all week. When she's sick she doesn't sleep well unless she sleeps in our bed with us, which means my husband and I don't get much sleep. I went to bed late due to taking care of her and planned on sleeping in a little. I woke up before my alarm went off then headed to the bathroom, looked at the time on my phone, and saw that I had a bunch of missed calls and texts. The shower in our bathroom had frosted windows and I noticed an orange glow, and I thought that was really weird.

My oldest daughters live in Oroville and Chico, and they were texting me saying, "Mom, Paradise is being evacuated!" I was barely awake, trying to figure out what was going on. I saw lots of missed calls from my parents. I went to the bedroom, and I started shaking my husband to wake him up. I told him, "There's a fire, Paradise is being evacuated, I'm not even shitting you."

He immediately sat up and looked at the time. He went straight to Cal Fire on his computer and tried to get as much information as he could, but official information was coming in so much slower than the fire was progressing. We didn't get any official evacuation calls, just concerned friends and family.

My parents called again and said that they were leaving and that the fire was on their side of town. We lived on the west side of town, and they lived on the east side. I got a text from one of my best friends who lived in the upper-middle part of town on Rocky Lane. She said there was a fire there. She said we needed to leave.

My husband and I were so confused. Was there a fire bug? Why are there fires in so many places across town? What was happening? Oddly enough, we didn't get a knock on our door from our neighbors, but they were outside packing and trying to figure out what was happening as well. There was so much debris falling from the sky that it sounded like rain and freaked out our cat, who took off and didn't come back that day (found safe in the same area forty-three days later with only minor singeing of his whiskers). We were talking to one of our neighbors, and a big chunk of smoldering ember fell out of the sky at our feet. I stamped it out. My neighbor said, "Preserve life, you need to leave. Preserve life." I will always remember that.

I called my new boss, who had only been there for two days because she took over for another manager. She told me not to come in and to get out of town. About this time the power went out. It was so dark we had to turn on our battery-powered camp lanterns to see anything inside. I was frantically grabbing pictures and mementos in the dark. My husband and I were arguing about leaving. He said we needed to get out ASAP.

I grabbed my daughter's backpack and dumped it out in the hallway. I thought I'd clean that up when I came back home. My husband told her to get everything she cared about and put it in that backpack. She had one backpack full of toys and another with clothes. I told my husband to get his guns and his guitars, but he didn't. One of his rifles was one that his dad built for him when he was sixteen. Thank goodness he grabbed our computer towers, because those had all of our pictures of our youngest daughter on them.

By the time we were done getting what we could out of the apartment, it was too dark to see into the garage to get to the totes of my twenty-five- and twenty-six-year-old daughters' stuff. This included sonogram tapes, baby books, first haircuts, and baby teeth. I had favorite bottles that were theirs and favorite outfits and baby blankets. Two years earlier, my mom had given me my grandfather's one-hundred-year-old christening gown and other sentimental things of his.

My husband was loading his car and I, mine, when I realized that I had almost no gas in it. I had been planning on getting gas that day when I got off work (I worked in town so just a two-minute commute). He had a gas can in the garage, and we got about three gallons in and figured that would do; we needed to hurry.

At this point it had been about two hours since we had woken up, but it didn't seem like it because of how crazy everything was. We lived just off Skyway on Honey Run Road. Skyway was absolutely packed with cars when we tried to leave. I was thinking, we aren't going to be able to get across! I remember how weirdly quiet it was as we pulled up to the stop. No one was screaming or panicking or honking their horns. The only real noise was the wind and explosions off in the distance.

We were let into traffic pretty quickly. Normally people aren't so quick to do so. I tried to stay as close as possible to my husband in front of me. Right when I got onto Skyway and I saw it, I realized what was happening and almost turned around to go back and get my stuff in the garage. I knew it was bad and that I'd never see my town the same again.

We were forced to escape driving the wrong way down Skyway. They had opened both sides up for outgoing traffic, but a power pole had fallen across the normal way out and traffic had to be funneled back down to the two normally incoming lanes. As we were heading down Skyway, I kept looking at the pine needles on my windshield from the wind and thinking, these are going to catch on fire and I will be screwed. I thought for sure the numerous burning power poles were going to fall on us. I saw people in the back of cars, trucks, and motor homes, and a couple people on bicycles as well.

We were just about out of it, and I saw a broken-down PT Cruiser and a guy standing out there, and I wanted to stop and give him a ride. If I stopped, I would either get rear-ended or I would lose my husband. I felt bad that I couldn't stop. He was under his hood trying to figure out what was wrong. We made it through Chico without stopping anywhere and continued on toward my in-laws' house in Browns Valley. We stopped at a little gas station near there to get gas, but I don't really even remember stopping. We've been with my in-laws ever since.

# Julie's Reflections

**What was the worst part of your experience?**

The worst part of my experience—well, there's so much. I would say losing my family history, history as in all of my family heirlooms, pictures, and keepsakes. I had already lost my grandparents when I was young. Losing the things that my grandfather built was awful. Losing my grandparents' home. Memories of gathering on their lawns in the summer, making ice cream and having parties, going to my grandparents' church, and having reunions and weddings there. There are just so many things in that town, and it's like the history is just gone. I can't point out to my kids where I fell and broke my collarbone. I can't say that's the church I went to and that's where I learned how to drive a stick shift, or this is the house I used to live in. It's not just my own personal history, but the town history that hurts. I've been there my whole life, and it hurts to have it all gone.

**Given the chance, what do you think you would do differently?**

If I could have done anything differently, I would have had my stuff more organized and ready to go in case of an emergency.

**What did you learn as a result of the fire?**

I've learned that even though the event is over, the trauma is still there. People expect you to be better after a certain amount of time. As my mom and I say, the fire still burns two years later. It still burns.

### What is your current situation?

I have a hard time working at the market I transferred to. The people aren't kind. It's not how the people were in Paradise. My husband and I have gone to great lengths to ensure our daughter continues her education in Paradise regardless of the fact that we currently live just over fifty miles away.

### How has the experience of the fire affected your family members?

My mom and dad's house was the only one still standing out of my entire family. The way my dad built the gate was what saved the house from the fire that burned the outbuildings and the landscaping and part of the roof. The fire reached the latch, and the gate fell down because of the way it was built. My mom feels so guilty—survivor's guilt. She wishes it would have just burned, too. It's been hard to watch my parents struggle with emotions and wondering if they are making the right decision to stay in town. This is a time they should be enjoying retirement instead of dealing with all of this. Most of my extended family all lived in town. Now they are spread out all over, and we don't get to see each other.

### How do you feel now?

I feel stuck. I am stuck. I am sleeping in an RV at my in-laws' home, with no air conditioning, with current fires going on, and the only way to get air is to have the windows open. I sleep with smoke coming in. I was doing OK when the smoke was down low because it looked like fog. You can't escape it, and I was having nightmares because of it, and it makes me angry. I ask my husband, is this our life now? Is fire our life? And the process to get back home is happening a lot slower than I want. I have to wait until the lawsuit ends in order to move back up there due to our finances.

### What do you miss about Paradise?

I used to get annoyed that I couldn't go anywhere without bumping into someone I knew, and now I really miss that. I miss what I had, and I have an appreciation for that now. As I have said before, it doesn't matter where you worked or where you lived, for the most part, the people of Paradise treated you with the same respect.

### What are some of your triggers?

The Ron Howard documentary, *Rebuilding Paradise*, was very triggering for me. Not because it was very bad or anything. I just know the town so well that seeing everything like that was and still is very difficult for me. The lawsuit and COVID-19 all stirred up the emotions again, and I feel kicked in the gut. Smelling smoke or hearing sirens really puts me on edge.

### How do you cope with the experience?

When I talk about it, it's almost like it's not real. I try to connect with it and maybe feel it more, but I think that I just don't want to.

# Clinician's Corner
# Survival Mode and Grief/Loss

The tragedy that Julie and her family experienced is what therapists consider a big T trauma. This type of trauma is defined as any event or circumstance that threatens or has the perceived threat of life or limb. This means the human mind detects or feels like the human body is threatened and possible death is imminent. Julie describes feeling as if she is still in a mental fog. She also describes a sense of loss of time and even space. These missing pieces to her lived memory of that fateful day are extremely common in trauma.

Brain fog is a very normal response to trauma and posttraumatic stress disorder (PTSD). Brain fog occurs when the mind goes into a fight-flight-freeze response in an attempt to protect the body from harm. Within the human brain, there are areas called the amygdala (pronounced *uh-mig-dala*). There is one located in the right hemisphere, and one located in the left hemisphere of the brain. The amygdala is the brain's trauma center, and it is in this area that the fight-flight-freeze response occurs. As in Julie's story, as soon as her mind registered that there was an imminent threat and that she and her family had to evacuate in order to save their lives, her amygdala function took control, and the frontal lobe of her brain, which is also her conscious mind, took a back seat. This function is called the amygdala hijack, and it is where your "system" is functioning strictly from survival mode. The amygdala activates this fight-or-flight response without any initiative from you. When that part of your brain senses danger, it signals your brain to pump stress hormones, preparing your body to either fight for survival or to flee to safety (Moyer, 2019).

Because the frontal lobe has been temporarily disabled during the amygdala hijack function, it can sometimes be very difficult for people to think clearly, make sound and rational decisions, and even control their responses to people, places, and things. Once there is no longer a physical threat to the body, the frontal lobe slowly comes back online and joins the rest of the brain to try to process the traumatic event. Since the frontal lobe was not in control during the event, some memories or pieces to the trauma story can sometimes not be accessible. This means that the conscious mind may not be able to remember everything that happened during the trauma. This is brain fog.

Visualize working on a project with another person. You both are responsible for completing this project, but neither one of you talks to or communicates with the other in any way. You both have an idea of what the project is, but you have no clue what the other person is doing on their end. Somehow you are supposed to finish the project together. This is the same dynamic between the frontal lobe and the amygdalae (plural). They both are working together but, in the moment of trauma and survival mode, they do not always communicate with each other.

This can sometimes be very upsetting for survivors who, days, weeks, months, or even years after a trauma, still cannot remember certain memories or facts about the event. We want to normalize this for you. It is your mind's way of protecting you and accepting the idea that you may not be able to remember everything. This is key to healing from trauma. It's OK if you cannot remember certain aspects of your trauma. It does not mean there is anything wrong with you; it means that your mind's protective function did its job correctly.

If you are experiencing brain fog, or if you feel like your memories of the trauma are surreal, it is important to ground yourself. When a trauma occurs and the mind goes into a fight-flight-freeze response, essentially the focus is on "outside the body" experiences, similar to an out-of-body experience. By grounding yourself, you can start to bring your thoughts and feelings back to your body. There are various techniques to help ground you in order to regain control over your mind. Meditation, yoga, and even simple stretching can center you back into yourself again, helping you connect your mind and body. Going for a walk or any other physical activity is a great way to get your body moving, and helps you connect back into yourself again.

To help with brain fog and your traumatic experience, it is important to have patience with yourself. It can be easy to be too hard on yourself for not being "fixed" or "healed" or even affected by the trauma. The most important lesson to take from this information is to hold space for your healing and give yourself time, patience, and grace. Healing takes time, and each person is different in how their minds process traumatic experiences.

Another aspect to Julie's story is the tremendous loss of memories, sentimental family valuables, and irreplaceable family heirlooms. Julie struggled to try to save as much of her and her family's valuables and personal items as possible. As you have just learned, when the mind is in survival mode, making reasonable and sharp decisions can sometimes be near impossible. Many items that Julie lost were passed down through her family's generations. In a traumatic event such as a fire, when family items, valuables, and important documents or memories are lost, there is most likely a period of grieving that must be experienced. As with the loss of a loved one, the process of grief and loss for the life that Julie knew is messy, sporadic, and most important, normal.

Grief is a nonlinear process, meaning there is no defined step one, step two, step three, and so on. It is common for survivors of trauma to bounce back and forth between many different emotions. Julie is not only grieving the loss of personal possessions, she is also grieving the loss of her home, her community, her town, and the life she knew. Julie essentially lost a part of her identity, if not much of her identity. You can find a Grief and Loss Symptom Checklist in the resources page here: www.SiftingThroughTheAshesResources.com

There are five common stages to grief and loss: Denial, Anger, Bargaining, Depression, and Acceptance (Kübler-Ross, 1969). Each one has their own substage that we will discuss in this section. Whatever stage you may be in or coming out of, the one thing we want you to understand is that it is absolutely normal and quite common. If you find yourself feeling stuck in a stage or substage, that is also normal. It is important that you give yourself time, patience, and a lot of grace through your healing journey. There are no time frames for processing and healing grief and loss.

Let's take a closer look at the stages of grief and their substages. Denial is sometimes considered the first stage of grief and loss because it is the mind's way of minimizing the pain of the loss. Because the loss is potentially so emotionally overwhelming, denial also attempts to "slow down" the processing of the loss as a means of protection. Within the stage of denial, we sometimes see substages such as *shock* or feeling *numb*. These substages are vital responses to the loss, and they work to protect us from becoming completely overtaken by the severity of our emotions. It can take some time for our minds to adjust to the sense of loss, so again it is important that you treat yourself kindly as you process your loss and grief.

Anger is the next common stage of grief. Anger can often be seen as masking of the pain and sorrow from the denial stage. Anger is looked at in therapy as a secondary emotion, meaning that if we dissect the anger, the components that make up anger are the deeper emotions attempting to be expressed. For example, if the loss of a loved one is too painful, your mind may express that loss in anger, and maybe even resentment, because for your mind, anger is easier to feel than pain and loss. Within this stage, you can often experience substages such as emotional outbursts, fear, and even panic. These experiences are normal to the process of grief, but not everyone will experience these substages in the same way. These emotional responses are your brain's way of processing the heaviness of the loss and attempting to make sense of it.

Bargaining is a common stage where anyone who is experiencing grief may think about what they could have done differently or visualize the past with a "what if" or "if only" internal dialogue. During grief and loss, you may feel emotionally helpless and vulnerable, and bargaining is your system's way of trying to regain control over the situation. If someone is carried by faith, they may attempt to negotiate with God or their higher power or make promises in return for relief from the pain. Bargaining and negotiation are natural responses to circumstances where you have no control over the loss.

Depression is another stage of the grief process. This stage is different in that it can be considered more of a "silent stage," whereas anger and bargaining are more "active or functioning" stages. Depression is considered a "silent" stage because many people report feeling foggy, confused, heavy, or just stuck in their pain, which can cause some people to withdraw and become isolated. Whereas the first three stages of grief are more outwardly expressed, those who are in the depressive stage of grief may feel guilt or the need to be alone. These substages can be considered common to depression, but not everyone will experience them. If you are in the depressive stage of grief and feel you are having a hard time moving through it, reaching out and seeking support from a mental health professional will likely help you feel less alone and provide you with the tools to cope with your loss in a healthy way.

Acceptance is seen as the final stage of grief. Acceptance does not always mean that it is a "happy" or "improved" stage of grief. It just means that you have found a way within your mind to see your loss as a part of your narrative and that you have chosen to move forward through processing your loss the best way you know how. Within this final stage, hope, strengths, and new life experiences are often achieved as a way to forge a "new normal" so you can move forward with life, not as a different person but the same you, just with a deeper level of experience. We see this stage in action by the mother who starts a charity in the name of the child she lost, or in the community park that was built to honor a soldier lost in combat. It is in this stage that our minds make meaning, big or small, of the loss and generate creativity within to honor the loss.

While the stages of grief appear defined and linear, in reality they are not. As you read in Julie's story, the expectation of how to get through an event like this can be overwhelming. In fact, those who are not experiencing the trauma and loss may not have a full understanding as to the severity of your process, and that's OK. Your process is your process, and you do not need to explain your process to anyone else. Allowing yourself to travel the road of grief and loss and allowing it to be messy and nonlinear, with no expectations of length of time, will yield less resistance to healing. It can be helpful to reach out for support from a mental health provider or support group if you feel you need a little extra help.

# LACEY'S STORY
## Escaping Paradise

It was a normal Thursday workday. My husband was a high school teacher in Paradise, and our daughter was a student. My oldest son slept in from working late the day before as a landscape designer. I worked as a clinic nurse and headed out the door at 6:30 a.m. to be in Oroville by 7 a.m.

I worked for an hour and then was asked to do the screening desk as that nurse had to be at an appointment. She left the building and then immediately called me and told me to come outside right away. I left the desk, walked out the back, and met my coworker in the parking lot. She pointed north and said, "Look! I don't know what's going on, but you should call your family." I ran back inside, got to the desk, and called my younger son, who worked from home.

I told him that something big was going on. There was lots of smoke. I told him to make sure his brother was up and get the cats inside. While I was speaking, my boss appeared in the doorway and said, "You live in Paradise, don't you?" I said yes, and she told me to go now and evacuate my family.

"But I'm working the desk . . ."

"Just go now," she said.

I returned to my phone call with my son and told him to get the cats in the carriers and put photo albums in the car and get out. He said my husband and our daughter had just gotten home from the school and were packing. I told him not to wait, but to get a few things and leave. We decided if I didn't make it into town, we would meet in Chico in the Costco parking lot.

I headed for the parking lot and drove out of Oroville and made it into Paradise by 9 a.m. The valley was warm and sunny, but Paradise looked like a dark and stormy day. It felt strange outside, but we had evacuated several times before, so we figured we'd be home later that day or maybe the next day.

My husband and kids were loading family videos, photo albums, and guitars into our van. The cats were caged and stuck in my car. I grabbed a change of clothes, some toiletries, and five bowls with a bag of Granola and a carton of almond milk, thinking at least we'd have one meal we didn't have to buy elsewhere. We all agreed to head out and, if separated, meet up in the Costco parking lot in Chico.

Leaving home at 9:15 a.m., we felt fairly calm; after all, we'd done this a few times. This time the sky was dark gray and not brown like in times past, so I figured the fire wasn't close. The traffic along Elliott at the end of our cul-de-sac was bumper-to-bumper and not moving much. My second son, twenty-two years old, was driving our Dodge van with our photos, videos, and guitars. He was the first one let onto the main road. Our daughter, seventeen, and I, with our four cats, followed but were separated by several cars. Then my husband with our oldest son, twenty-six, merged into traffic in his old car.

The traffic was very stop-and-go. We sat on that half-mile section of road for more than an hour. The sky darkened to black. The cats hated the car, but they were strangely quiet. My daughter was sending texts to friends to see if they were OK. Her friend's mother was a doctor at the hospital, and she was refusing to leave because she had patients. Her daughter was crying on the phone to my daughter, saying she saw their house burning down. She was afraid her mother was stuck at the hospital. She herself was OK and being driven out by someone else. They lived over by the hospital. My daughter was crying in sympathy. This was getting too real, or unreal.

Our second son sent me a text saying the van gas tank was on empty. I called him and said if he needed to pull over and get out to leave the van and come find us. We were still on Elliott behind him. Cell service dropped. There was no way to call or text. My husband didn't have a cell phone. I had no idea where he was. I assumed he was on the same road, just somewhere behind me.

People were walking and running along the road with dogs and blankets, holding a bag or two. They were making much better time than we were. I'm glad I didn't know what the booming sounds were. I found out they were exploding propane tanks that were getting closer. I'm glad I couldn't see the flames that were just around the corner from where we were stuck in traffic. I commented to my daughter that I was so thankful that, in spite of the traffic, people seemed to be calm. No one was honking or yelling.

There was spotty cell service for a minute, and a text came through from our son saying he was leaving the van. I replied that we were on Elliott and would wait for him. He didn't get that last reply. We finally got closer to Skyway, and I pulled into a church parking lot on the right and planned to wait for our son. We waited, and within fifteen minutes or so my husband drove by and pulled over when he saw me. I explained that our son ran out of gas and had to abandon the van and run for it, but I didn't see any vehicles on the side of the road, and I was near the end of Elliott. My husband said for us to go on to the meeting place and he would wait for our son.

My daughter and I pulled back into the line of cars, turned onto Skyway, and headed west toward Chico. Traffic was still stop-and-go. It was dark as night, only now we could see buildings in the near distance on fire on both sides of us. I was wondering if it was just on one side of town and how it was spreading. The smoke seemed to be coming from everywhere.

We approached the south end of Paradise near the Adventist Health Clinic on the right, and there was a downed live power line snaking around on the road. The road was full of cars trying to merge from all directions and going straight was not an option. The woods were on fire, the buildings all around were on fire, and the live wire and blowing flames prevented us from going through. A car up ahead was veering to the left and drove into the oncoming traffic lanes. I followed, as that seemed the only option. Another car with the same idea nearly plowed into us, but thankfully was a near miss.

We drove in extreme darkness, with blowing embers showering us. There were flames literally a few feet away. The heat was so powerful the window glass was hot. I saw my daughter in the rear-view mirror, and she was calm but had tears streaming down her cheeks. The four cats, stuffed two to a carrier, remained perfectly silent. I started praying, or I guess I continued praying. I was basically asking God to not let us be either baked alive or fried outside. It seems strange, but that's exactly what I was thinking. I was also praying that if it was our time to die, then to let it be both of us together and super quick.

We were still trundling along slowly, but thankfully not stop-and-go. Cars were pulling to the side as they were catching fire. The car in front of me had its taillights melting. The fire and ember shower continued. I didn't know if someone would need help or need to hop in, but in the line of cars there was no stopping. I knew if I pulled over to try to help someone, we would be stuck, too. Visibility was poor. We could see just the car in front of us and the ones on the side of the road.

It was past the main drama. I suggested my daughter take a video of the scene out her window with her phone. She got a video clip from the left side of the car, opposite the side the wind was blowing. Flames on the ground were evident, but the blowing and burning was to the right of us.

I prayed all the way out of there. The farther we went, the sky began to lighten. I felt hopeful. We picked up speed, and the smoke was higher so that we could see ahead. We were still alive. I felt so thankful. I looked to the other traffic lane, the one going west that we were supposed to be in, and I saw my son drive past on that part of the road. Yay, he made it too! I followed a vehicle that crossed over at a clear point to the road going in the correct direction. Others were following me.

I had our daughter try to send a text to our son. He replied that he was with Daddy. I said to tell Daddy that we drove through fire, but it's OK, he'll make it. As we approached Chico, there were hundreds of people on the side of the roads looking at all the cars coming down the hill, searching for family and friends. They were cheering as each car drove past. It was such a wonder. We got to Costco just after noon. It took us three hours to make a twenty-minute trip. Having to use the bathroom, we went in, then sent our son a text to meet us at the food court.

There were several people sitting in the food court without food. Blank looks on faces. I knew they came from Paradise. We sat down to wait, and then it seemed like suddenly people all around us were talking to each other and telling their story. There was a lady I recognized from church. I didn't know her, but we knew who each other was. She came up to me and said, "I really need a hug." So, I gave her one. She cried and said she'd driven through fire. I knew. I told her we had, too.

Then an older couple came over to where my daughter and I were sitting and waiting, and they asked if we were from Paradise. We said yes. They explained that they had come to Chico early to do shopping, and asked us what happened in Paradise and if they could go home. I told them of the fire, smoke, darkness, and flames all over town. I told them they couldn't drive up there. That's all I knew. They went from table to table, asking for information. I could hear stories of people having their clothes on fire and not knowing it, of getting their animals out, of seeing their homes burn. The feeling in the air was excited, like someone's sports team making an amazing winning play. People felt triumphantly relieved to be alive and to talk about it. My husband and two sons found us and told their story. It's the biggest event that has ever happened, and the most danger we've all been in. Everyone was hyped up.

Then the question came. Where would we go now? Our daughter said she got two texts from friends telling us to come to their homes—our whole family. I was amazed. Before we even considered what to do next, the answer was provided. We replied to one of the friends and said we appreciated the invitation, and we would be there soon. We asked if they needed anything from Costco.

We arrived at the family home of our friends. They had invited several families over. Everyone talked and retold stories. I contacted the clinic where I work to tell them I was OK, but I wouldn't be back at work that day. They said that I needed to take the rest of the week and the next week off and figure things out. I really had no idea what that meant until reality hit the next day.

Everyone at the house stayed awake looking at rental sites, checking in with family, sitting and staring. I applied online to several rental agencies, figuring that we might need it. The family allowed us to use their daughter's room, and our four cats stayed in the room, too. By the way, there was not a single litter box and scoop to be had anywhere in the area of Chico. We tried every store.

We were loaned an old camper that was delivered to the friend's backyard within two weeks of our landing there. Another family had a trailer in the front yard. We all shared a tiny bathroom in the house. The camper bathroom was very limited in its use and the toilet leaked all over the camper carpet, so we didn't use it. It was very cold. The roof leaked over our bed. The tarp was wonderful. We shared that space with our cats all winter.

We had no idea if our home had survived. A friend with a press pass was able to get into town a couple of weeks after the fire. She took photos of people's properties and posted them on a website. We were able to determine that at least the front part of our house still existed. We had no idea if it was livable. The next time we went back to Paradise was nearly a month and a half later, with a police escort, to visit our property. Our house stood, along with our right-hand neighbor's and the across-the-street neighbor's. There had been fourteen houses on our street, and now there were five standing. It was pretty amazing considering most other neighborhoods were decimated.

We went inside cautiously to get a few clothes. The smell was overwhelming. Just opening the front door gave me a severe headache for the rest of the day. We were allowed about five minutes to check on things and then were escorted out of town again.

It was four long months before we were able to live there. It was a disaster area with contaminated water, debris, and heavy work trucks everywhere driven by out-of-towners who could care less about the survivors. They were there to make money as fast as they could. Our insurance paid for a house cleaner that basically gave it a once-over and did not do a thorough job.

My son and I are asthmatics, and we had severe attacks that didn't go away. Instead of taking my rescue inhaler once a week or so, I was needing it more than six times per day without real effect. All the soft furnishings and carpeting, which insurance said only needed to be cleaned, still reeked of the chemical smoke smell, and had to be removed and replaced, mainly at our own cost. Getting back to some semblance of normal took a long time. Just the insurance, work hassles, records and receipts, bills and taxes, and quirky camper issues kept us more than busy.

We could stay strong and busy for just so long before we crashed. Having all my friends, most of my church family, and my husband's job location move away was very difficult. Being left behind and living in a dirty disaster area was more difficult and took a toll on my health. Between asthma and hormones, stress, weight gain, anxiety, worry for the future, and grief for my friends, it all piled up and I found myself crying all the time.

My job can be extremely stressful during normal times, and we were short a registered nurse for several months. I kept telling human resources I was having a difficult time coping with the workload by myself. On most days, I did the work of two RNs, and Fridays I did the job of three. HR kept asking me to wait and be patient. No one had applied for the open RN position. After my stress level had reached a sobbing-without-stopping point, the provider I saw at the clinic ordered me to take two weeks off for mental health. I took one day off. There was no way I could afford to take the time off financially or to lump the workload onto my coworker. I just couldn't do it. I continued working at my job, which I was thankful to have.

Many of our patients were from Paradise and had lost everything. They would call my screening desk for medication refills and to be seen for panic attacks, anxiety, stomachaches, headaches, etc. Several would cry on the phone, and I would listen and let them get their story out. Some people would react with very short tempers. When things at the clinic weren't happening as fast as they'd like or not meeting their needs, they would blow up and cuss me out on the phone. I would listen and let them rant. Sometimes, but not always, I would tell them I understood or that I could imagine their frustration. They would rant some more and ask how I could possibly understand, and I would tell them that I went through it, too.

I was finally able to get some help, through Heartstrings Counseling, for me and two of my kids. They were also having a hard time emotionally. My husband seemed to be doing OK. He gets his therapy through doing yard work and rebuilding some of the things in our place that did burn down.

Our younger son told us that after the van ran out of gas, he got out and pushed it down the road and into another church's parking lot. He ran through the darkness and smoke toward what he thought was the right direction. He climbed the fence to the graveyard and ran through that. He then climbed over the fence on the other side and found Elliott. My husband was waiting at the same church parking lot where I left him. He had no way to get in touch with our other son or anyone else. He had no idea if our son would have to get a ride with someone else just to get out, or if he would still be coming to find him. If our son was closer, he knew he couldn't stay either. But he wouldn't leave our son. He stayed, and thankfully our son came and found him.

They drove through the fire and met us in Chico. That was a very hard thing. Months later, our younger son would have some stress issues as well, such as jaw clenching/TMJ issues, and gut reactions to the smell of smoke or seeing a flame. Counseling wasn't an option for him as there were no more available counselors or fire victims' sessions open. He is doing better now. I've shared with him things I've learned.

Incidentally, the van with our photos, family videos, and guitars was found in the parking lot where our younger son had pushed it. Nothing inside was damaged. The van didn't work anymore and smelled horrendous. We got no help or compensation for that loss, but we are so thankful for the miracle of those personal items being safe. Of course, we all felt guilty to have such things when it seemed everyone else lost their things.

We continue to have that guilt. Also, we didn't have the freedom to move on like so many did. With a mortgage on a house that was in a disaster area and with jobs still active, we didn't think we'd have a chance to sell our house for anything. We couldn't leave, but it was hard to stay.

Things are better with the house and the town. It's still lonely, but we are very grateful to have a place to live. The most important things we learned from this experience are how precious family and friends are. Stuff is just stuff. People are resilient and can adapt when they try. It's OK to grieve, but we have to allow ourselves to grow beyond that. New things can seem scary, but it's part of life, and we can get good at doing and learning new things. Even in the worst and most uncertain of times, we are never alone, and our needs will be provided for. Remember to choose thankfulness and joy.

# Lacey's Reflections

### *What was the worst part of that experience for you?*

The worst experience the day of the fire was when my second son had to abandon the vehicle he was driving with all of our important papers and baby videos and everything in it. He had to run and find us, and we weren't sure if he was going to find us. We didn't know how long it would take and if we should leave or not leave. We weren't sure if he was going to catch a ride with somebody else. We were surrounded by fire, and he was running from one street several blocks away. He was hopping tall fences, running through a graveyard, running to the other side, and then running down another road to try to find our car in traffic. He did find us, but we lost cell connection and there was no way to communicate. My husband waited and he said, "You take our daughter and the cats and go. I will wait for him."

### *What would you have done differently?*

That is hard. I think I would have brought some extra clothes. I brought five bowls and a box of cereal in case we got hungry. I don't think I would have changed anything. Everything worked so perfectly even though it was crazy. It was scary, and it was slow-moving. I don't think there was anything we could have done differently. I just wish we had a few more items of clothing that we didn't have to buy.

### What have you learned from this experience?

Everybody really does have a story, whether or not they went through a trauma or tragedy like this. Events can shape a person's outlook on life, but a person can choose. We could have turned on each other, but we turned toward each other. There were times my husband was weak, and I could support him, and there were other times I was falling apart, and he supported me. For our kids, it was hard on them, really hard. All of our needs were met. We learned again that priorities shift. Things that are important are not really that important. Family, friendships, relationships with other people are so much more valuable, and when that gets divided and people have to leave, it takes effort to make new friends. And, if you want that, you have to push yourself a little bit and get it.

### How have the recent fires affected you?

It was not mandatory but recommended for us to evacuate Paradise. We did. We knew the drill—load of this, load of that, get the cats in the carrier, and let's go. We had the same meeting place. It was like a rerun of a bad dream. Then we got down there and didn't know what to do; it was different. Before, friends were saying, "Come to our house," but this time there was nothing, just crickets. There was no outreach—no support—and what do we do? It triggered a lot. Every time we smelled smoke, every time we heard reports of fires somewhere, I would get anxious. I would say, "We have to move, we have to move. We cannot continue to go through this every year." It was a big trigger.

### What are you still struggling with?

I think every summer we face the threat of our power being turned off. We face dry winds that are dangerous to this area. We always face the risk of this happening again. I feel I would like to move, and it is not the right time career-wise. I really want to get chickens, but how do you evacuate with chickens? Hotels would not take chickens. I struggle with being surrounded by dead trees. It is a fear factor. It is a residue in the area of the fire. There's always the threat of fire in the summer.

### What keeps you going?

Taking it one day at a time. I do have tools to use when I feel anxious. I do feel a lot happier. I do still have things to be thankful for and practice thankfulness. I practice mindful breathing and other techniques. This has boosted my resilience. I discovered I am incredibly resilient. We all have been resilient, which I would not have thought. Having joy. It is not just a choice; it is something you keep. One day at a time.

### If you could give another survivor any advice, what would it be?

There are so many clichés that you could say, but it would all still hurt. Recognize the hurt is real. The loss is real. But you have to let go and move forward. You have to let go of the things you lost and just move forward.

# Clinician's Corner
# Shared Experience and Human Resilience

One of the main themes throughout Lacey's story is how the community came together to share their experience with one another. This type of community support can be common when a population shares a traumatic or negative experience. While each individual has their own personal experience, the population as a whole also works together to survive. As you have just read, Lacey struggled with wanting to stop and pull over to the side of the road to help those who had become stuck. The hard truth is that if she did pull over, she would have likely gotten stuck too, which threatened her safety and the safety of her children.

This sense of needing or wanting to help others seems to come naturally to Lacey. She is a nurse, and helping people is something she was doing every day. It would have been second nature for her to stop to make sure others were OK.

The sense of comradery and celebration when cars made it down the hill to safety is another example of the community supporting each other through this shared trauma. In those moments of escaping the fire with literally what they had in their cars, each of the Paradise residents was fighting for their own lives, some with their families, some alone, but all of them only had themselves to rely on to get through the fire. It was do-or-die, and that type of situation can feel extremely lonely and frightening. Once they were out of harm's way, that close sense of community was able to return when they needed it most.

As families reunited and survivors were able to eat and drink, each person's nervous system was able to calm and find a level of normalcy again. The beginning of the processing of what just happened can often allow those who have shared the trauma to create bonds. There was no one else, at that moment, who could understand what Lacey and her family had just gone through like those who had gone through it, too. These bonds created by trauma can often serve multiple functions: validation, identity, and meaning.

Human resilience is another factor we see reflected in Lacey's story. Resiliency is the human capacity to thrive and adapt in the face of tremendous adversity and stress, such as the Camp Fire. Research has shown that resiliency is more common than you might think (Riopel, 2021). Having resiliency does not mean an absence of pain or struggle; resiliency means that in the face of that pain and struggle you were able to overcome adversity and thrive. If you are having difficulty overcoming and moving past your trauma, that does not mean that you cannot learn to strengthen your resiliency. You most certainly can. Resiliency can be learned through developing thoughts, actions, and behaviors that move you through your stressful or traumatic experience.

The construct of resiliency is built upon numerous factors which we will talk about here. These factors include having good problem-solving skills, having good communication skills, having the capacity to make realistic plans and the ability to carry out those plans, having confidence in one's strengths and abilities, and, most important, being able to manage your thoughts, emotions, and impulses in a healthy way. We will further discuss three of these resilience factors and provide tools and/or guidance on how you can strengthen these factors within yourself. Our intention is to help you heal and grow your resiliency so that you can continue along your healing journey. With any tools, interventions, or guidance that you receive from this book or any other outside resources, please take what resonates and leave what does not.

One of the most important resiliency factors in the healing of trauma is the ability to manage thoughts, emotions, feelings, and impulses. This is one of the more significant factors because how each of us manages our mind, body, and spirit is solely in our own control. We do not have the ability to control others' actions, behaviors, and attitude. We can only control our own. Being able to identify and manage the thoughts, emotions, feelings, and impulses that you are experiencing is necessary to overcome and thrive through trauma, struggle, and adversity. Doing so with reason and healthy logic will allow you to stay in control and be empowered over your life. You can find our Human Resiliency Checklist on the resources page here:
www.SiftingThroughTheAshesResources.com

A healthy way to manage your emotions in order to strengthen your resiliency is to experience the emotion without becoming the emotion. Being able to experience an emotion and being able to stay in control of your response to the experience is a foundation in emotional regulation. We see emotional dysregulation often when someone is angry. Anger can be a very hard emotion to control, and it is common to see angry outbursts, hostility, violence, and other unhealthy reactions.

Emotional regulation is having a healthy response rather than an unconscious reaction to the emotional stimulus. A healthy response to anger could look something like this: "I am feeling really angry right now. I don't want to hurt my loved ones by yelling at them, so instead, I am going to go for a long walk and process my emotions." Another factor in building resilience is the ability to communicate effectively. In keeping with the example above, the ability to communicate to loved ones about how you are feeling and what you are thinking will put you in the perfect position to feel understood, feel validated, and to have your needs met. It could look like this: "I am feeling really angry right now. I don't want to hurt your feelings, so I am going to take a long walk and cool off so I can talk to you about my feelings later."

Having the ability to engage in healthy communication shows you can manage your emotions and, at the same time, respond with reasonable logic to your experience. A large part of strengthening resilience is controlling how you respond to adversity. Having effective, healthy communication also sets boundaries between you and other people so that your needs are met without projecting or deflecting shame, blame, or other judgments onto other people, possibly hurting their feelings. This is an important factor in strengthening resilience because, when faced with a trauma, negative experience, or adverse circumstance, our flight/fight/ freeze response will want to take over and function strictly on emotional reaction. Effective communication, in a way, brings a grounding presence to that emotional reaction. You can find our Healthy Communication Exercises on the resources page here:
www.SiftingThroughTheAshesResources.com

The last resiliency factor we will discuss is having confidence in your strength and abilities. It is absolutely possible to grow your confidence in yourself. Humans are amazingly resilient beings, and you are no exception.

Trusting that in the moment you need it, you are capable of managing yourself, controlling how you respond to your environment, and taking action accordingly to ensure you and your loved ones stay safe. You've got this! We believe in you!

You can strengthen these resiliency factors by practicing and working on your response to your environment each day, little by little. The first step is to recognize when you are stressed and what your stressors are. These may be large crowds, loud noises, feeling alone or isolated, or anything else that propels your body into the flight/fight/freeze response.

Once you know your stressors, you can better manage your reactions to them. The next step is to strengthen your mind and body's response to calming down and self-regulating. This can be done with meditation, exercise, mindfulness, or any other activity you find peace in. It is important to learn to self-soothe in order to train your mind to strengthen your relaxation response. The last step is to strengthen the positive feelings and your response to them. Finding people, activities, and environments that bring you humor, or joy, can help you connect with the more positive aspect of life, which helps build your resilience to life when it is less positive.

Working on these steps little by little will help you build your resilience, manage your emotions, and find empowerment over your life. As Lacey's story concluded, people are resilient and, with a little effort, new and uncertain circumstances can open the door to opportunities for growth and healing.

# CINDY'S STORY
## Paradise Lost

**I**woke up late for me. It was dark out. I was looking out the windows and I could hear cars going down the street. I looked across the street at our neighbor's house. The sky looked eerily silvery-grayish, and the trees held kind of an eerie feeling. I reached over to my husband and told him we needed to get up and get going. He kind of rumbled around and asked what time it was.

Something came over his phone. He got an evacuation warning about a fire in Concow. He kept saying he was getting notifications about the power being turned off due to the high fire conditions. I kept hearing cars on the streets. I turned on the television and we watched the coverage of the fire.

My husband called his sister and asked what they were doing. She said they were packing and getting ready to evacuate. We told her we would too and started packing. Before 10 a.m. the power went out, and it was hard to pack or get around in the dark. It was the first time we were in a situation where we had to have a to-go bag. My husband was not up and at 'em.

My husband was trying to get more information about the fire and I was in the house getting things ready to go. It was getting pretty scary. The sky was turning black. I looked outside and saw flames coming down the street. At that point, I said, "Oh, man, we need to leave, we need to go now."

There were embers coming down from the sky, and it was really windy. We decided to take my little car because his car was parked in the yard. We got the dog. It was really dark then, and we got in the car and pulled out of the garage. My husband asked if he could go back and clear the pine needles off the roof. I said, "No, we have to go now." We made a left turn and headed to Wagstaff, and there were a lot of cars.

A friend called 911 and said the fire was coming down the street and we had to evacuate immediately. There was fire on both sides of the street, and we could feel the heat. We heard exploding, and we inched our way down toward Skyway. We saw the fire trucks going down Skyway and all the cars being directed down Skyway. We chose to go on the farthest lane out, which was coming up on the side of the street going out of town. There were four lanes going out of town.

We inched our way. There was a motorcade of three cops that passed some cars that were abandoned due to the fire. We were not moving very fast but started moving a bit faster. A lot of people were out of their cars. It was pretty scary, and the dog was freaked out. We saw some trees on fire and a lot of cars on fire. When we saw all of the fire trucks, we knew the fire was coming our way. We knew they didn't have it under control. Everywhere there was fire. That was pretty devastating.

We went to Chico going down Skyway, and we made it in about three hours. Down at the bottom of the hill, we rushed through the smoke, and we were wondering where to go. They opened up one of the churches in Chico, and we decided to check in there.

Our dog knew something was very wrong. Every time my husband would leave my side, she became antsy and agitated. She was trying to figure out where he was. The church tried to take care of us, giving us water and food and offering us sheets, pillows, toiletries, towels, and basic clothing. It was pretty crazy. There was a situation where the bathrooms were backed up and they had to take us to a different place to use the bathroom. It was pretty chaotic. We didn't sleep well with the air mattresses. We didn't have a very restful night.

We decided to go to Southern California to stay with our friends. All of the people in the shelter were trying to find out some information. I couldn't deal with it, so I stayed away from it. But it kind of flashed across the news, and I tried to stay away from watching the news, but that's how I learned Paradise was lost.

By the time we got to our friends' home in Southern California, we checked on the CAL-Fire website to see what was gone and what was destroyed. It was maybe three days, and one of our neighbors contacted us. We learned our house was gone. The picture we got was my husband's car that was there, and the house was destroyed.

# Cindy's Reflections

### What was the worst part of that experience for you?

I think the feeling of competition, because there were so many people, the sheer numbers at the same place at the same time. We had to keep calm but also had to fight for resources. You had to fight for it.

### What would you have done differently?

I guess trying to be more prepared. Getting more. It's a hard thing to say.

### How have the recent fires affected you?

It set us back a lot. Even the dog looking at us as we were bringing our belongings to the car. She went back to wanting both of us in the same place. I was more aware of keeping less things and being more prepared and being ready. We continued to be vigilant and watch the signs. It hit me as part of a flashback.

### What have you learned from this experience?

That it is OK for people to see me with emotion. That my church family and other people are really supportive and there for us.

### What are you still struggling with?

Not being able to have a place. Being stuck because our other house hasn't started to rebuild, and all the things we have are not "ours." Everything is just temporary and not ours. Still being in a place where we haven't moved on.

### What keeps you going?

I guess knowing that other people still have the same ups and downs as me. I am not alone.

### If you could give another survivor any advice, what would it be?

I think finding a place to talk to other people about it really helps. We were not in a wildfire before. You need to define what you need to pack and take what you need. I learned that from this experience. Do not procrastinate. Be really patient with other people who have gone through it. I learned to ask for help. Understand the toll it takes on you and the images you see in your mind.

We learned it's important to keep moving and have something of a grounding to help. I would start writing a list and make sure the things that need to go are packed this time. That was hard for me personally. I thought I was stronger.

# Clinician's Corner
# Staying Grounded During
# Displacement and Somatic
# Therapy

One aspect that Cindy still struggles with is the continued displacement and feelings of being stuck due to a lack of housing, possessions, and a sense of home, or "ours" as she describes. These feelings are common and normal when a person experiences a loss of home and, in essence, a loss of self. While having these feelings, it is essential to stay grounded as a means of maintaining a sense of normalcy during a displacement. Here are a few ways you can ground yourself while feeling displaced.

One of the best ways to help you feel grounded when you are feeling displaced is to create a routine. This will allow you to cultivate normalcy in your life. Activities such as maintaining the same wake-up time in the morning, going for a walk after breakfast, having lunch at the same time every day, making a point to get errands done around the same time every day, and getting to bed at the same time every night can help you form new routines, new lifestyles, and a new "normal."

Forming new routines can help your body feel secure in knowing what is coming next. This is especially important when you have experienced life-changing circumstances such as a fire, a divorce, and even a pandemic. When you experience such circumstances, essentially your homeostasis, or stable equilibrium, is imbalanced, and it can feel detrimental to your innate survival mechanisms. Creating and maintaining new routines can help rebalance your homeostasis, which will allow you to feel more grounded and secure in life. This process can take time and patience, but the more you practice the routine the easier it can be to begin to feel settled and less displaced.

Another grounding technique is to go inward into your body. We talked about breathing and the benefits of breath work earlier. Breath work is great for calming your nervous system and feeling relaxed. We want to add the concept of somatic work to your breath work. One of the best remedies when you feel ungrounded and displaced is to anchor back into your body. Somatic work allows you to focus your attention on your body, get in touch with your deepest emotions, and understand how your body actually holds your emotions. The theory behind somatic work is that the sensations associated with past trauma may become trapped within the body and reflected in facial expressions, posture, muscular pain, or other forms of body language (GoodTherapy. Org, updated 2017). Your mind, body, spirit, and emotions are all connected and should be treated as a whole system approach.

The use of somatic therapy or practices in the processing of trauma can bring a deeper level of healing to your experience. As you learn to connect your body to your emotions, you can gain a deeper level of attunement that you may need at any given time or place. The whole point to any type of healing work is to know yourself better and to have an awareness about your needs so that you may then work to meet those needs. Somatic work is a wonderful way to show up for yourself in a way no one else can. Simply breathing into your body and becoming aware of your emotional experiences is a level of awareness that even a therapist cannot have. You have the powerful ability to connect back into yourself and know exactly where you are holding pain, trauma, and unresolved emotions. Working with a therapist who is experienced in somatic work can help you make sense of and work through your new awareness. You will get a chance to practice a bit of somatic work in just a little bit.

We recommend a book called *The Body Keeps the Score: Brain, Mind, and Body in the Healing of Trauma*, written by Bessel van der Kolk. In this book, van der Kolk describes the science of trauma in reshaping our body and our brain. He also describes the correlation between our emotional systems and how that is manifested in our bodies as disease, illness, and our capabilities for pleasure.

When our bodies are imbalanced and our mental and emotional states are dysregulated, an inner alarm system alerts us. We can create change in our bodies if we are ready to open ourselves up to our inner experience (van der Kolk, 2014).

Somatic work can help you focus back into your body and notice where in your body you are holding on to stress, tension, sadness, fear, trauma, survival, shame, and even forgiveness. Let us walk you through a somatic exercise. Read through the following process, and then take a moment to try it.

Sit in a comfortable position with your feet flat on the floor. As you get comfortable and settle into your body, close your eyes and take a few big, deep, slow breaths. Focus on your lungs taking in and releasing the air. As you inhale, visualize the air flowing into your body, expanding your chest cavity as large as it can expand. With each exhale, visualize all your negative thoughts and emotions flowing out of your body. With each inhale and exhale, you ground further into your body.

After a few minutes of breathing, visualize a scan of your body. Start from the top of your head and narrow your mental focus on each area of your body that you are scanning. Notice if there are any areas that "ping" for you. A "ping" can be a thought, a feeling in your gut, a color that you see in your mind, a wave of emotion, or even a physical sensation that may manifest for you. Once you locate a "ping" in an area of your body, sit in that place for a little bit. Notice what is coming up for you. It is important to note here that there is nothing you have to do with the information that comes up for you. Just acknowledge it. Sit with it and honor it.

The next step, once you have found and acknowledged the area that holds a charge for you, is to breathe healing into that area. Focus on the area of your body where you felt the thought, emotion, or sensation. Visualize yourself sending love, healing, and understanding into that area. As you do this visualization, notice how your body feels, any changes in your emotions, and any other sensations that you may feel. When you feel ready, open your eyes and come back to the present moment.

# LUCY'S STORY
## Survivor's Guilt

It started out like any other morning. It was windy, really windy, all night long. The time shifted the week before for Daylight Savings, so it was dark. We were adjusting to the time change. I got up at about 4:30 or 5 in the morning. I am an early riser, and I was only retired for a year, so I was in the habit of getting up really early.

I got up, fed the cat, got a cup of coffee, and read the newspaper. And it was dark, but it was supposed to be dark. The cat wanted to be let out after he ate, so I let him out the front door. The cat usually goes from our house to our neighbor's house across the street. He would hang out there and come back at night. I assumed he had gone across the street. I woke my husband up because he was going to be getting wood from the neighborhood.

PG&E was on Pentz Road, not very far from where we lived. They were taking down trees for fire purposes, and all of the wood was sitting there along the road. My husband was going down to get wood, and they didn't care if anyone was getting wood. That's all we used for home heat.

It just kept getting darker and darker. The sky was red, and I was watching the news. On TV, channel 12, they reported a ten-acre fire in Concow. I went about my business here, and in about ten to fifteen minutes, I checked the Butte County Fire and Accidents page on Facebook. Suddenly, that ten-acre fire was one hundred acres. That was in fifteen minutes. At that point, my husband came back and said he was pretty sure there was a fire coming our way.

The wind was blowing really hard, and he went ahead and dumped the wood. Then we took the pickup down and gassed up. My husband told me to keep watching the news and see what we could find out. It happened so fast. I kept watching the news. It kept getting darker, and the wind was howling, and the sky was red. The sky appeared redder.

After we gassed up the truck, my husband said, "We need to get out of here. There is a fire." We started packing stuff up. We were in survival mode. He backed the car up to the kitchen door, and we loaded both the pickup and the car. Fortunately, we kind of had everything organized because we had that situation before in 2008 where we had to evacuate. We had legal paperwork in drawers, so we simply took the drawers and the filing cabinet and put them in the back of the pickup, and we did get the reverse 911 call. I know a lot of people did not.

We kept trying to call our daughter, and it kept going to voicemail. We wanted to let her know there was a fire on the east side of town; she was on the west side of town. I wasn't too concerned about that since it was on this side, but we were still concerned about what was going on. I can't remember at what point, what zones were to evacuate. Finally, it was "evacuate the whole town."

We pretty much had everything packed. I went out to look for our cat, and I couldn't find him. I did not have time to look for him. I came back in, and my husband said he was going to unhook the travel trailer and take that with us with the pickup. He had the trailer on blocks for the winter. We were on a camping trip maybe two weeks before the fire.

I went out to help, but my husband told me I better go get our dog, Piper. She was running around and really antsy. I grabbed her and put her in the house and went out to help with the trailer. We could hear the embers hitting the metal parking shed. Cinders were dropping, and at that point we had to get out of there. I didn't care about the trailer. We just needed to get out of there and find someplace to stay. We needed to go, and we needed to go now. My husband insisted on getting the trailer out. He did. He got the trailer hooked up and came back in and made a quick sweep of everything.

I had a cockatiel in a big birdcage, and I said, "Buddy, you are on your own. I don't have any place I can put you." My car was packed, and I didn't think about the trailer and I could have put him in the trailer. I just covered him up, and my husband told me to grab some food so I threw some in a bag.

As we left, my husband said, "You better say goodbye to your house, because it is not going to be here."

I said, "I already said goodbye to the house."

At that point, I was thinking all of this stuff is replaceable. What is important is people's lives. So, we headed out. My husband was ahead of me in the pickup with the trailer. I looked across Bille Road, and everything was on fire. I couldn't believe it. Everything was burning—fences, trees, houses, and knolls.

We sat on the hill for a long time. No one would let us in on the road. Suddenly, a guy in one of the cars on Bille Road was distracted on his cell phone. I was on Virginia Street, and he didn't pull up, and my husband pulled in. We could tell the guy was really angry. We finally managed to get out on the street, and I can remember sitting there forever because it took forever for the cars to move, and the whole other side of the street was on fire.

From the side of the street I was on, I saw deer running off the road. They too were in survival mode. All of a sudden, people were walking and running on the sidewalks. There were kids in wagons. People were driving cars on the sidewalk. There was a lady, and I still feel terrible to this day, a grandma with a walker on the sidewalk. I thought, "Holy crap, I should have thrown a bunch of stuff out of the passenger seat and grabbed her and hauled her into the car." Why didn't I do it? I don't even know. I really feel so bad about that.

Traffic was moving slowly. We were just focused on getting out and trying to stay as calm as we could. Time was standing still. The traffic in both lanes was going in the same direction. My husband had already told me to watch his bumper and don't lose him. Whenever he made a lane change, I would make a lane change. Traffic was stopped in one lane but moving in the other lane. It is lucky I didn't run into the rear end of the trailer. But we finally almost got up to Clark and Bille. I could see the orange glow of the fire in the rearview mirror. We knew it had to be really close.

The other thing I remember was coming down the hill on Bille. We got stopped at Walgreens before we turned on Skyway, and it seemed like we sat there forever. It was black as night. It was like midnight, but all of a sudden the wind would blow the smoke away and we would see this big orange/red glow of the sun. We finally got on Skyway. Traffic stopped for a long,

long time. There was a policeman who came up to some of the cars. He told us if we were given the word, we should shut the vehicle off, get out of the car, and walk to Walgreens. He said they would break the doors and we would go in there for shelter.

Fortunately, the traffic started moving again. All of the lanes were full and trying to get out.

Then the cell center went out. Our daughter finally picked up the phone, so we could let them know all about the fire. They had been asleep. Her little girl was sick, so they were sleeping in. They had no idea about the fire. Eventually she rolled over and saw her cell phone and that she had fifteen messages. That was really frightening to lose cell service.

The scariest part was when we got down to Skyway to where our daughter lived off Honey Run, all we could see were flames coming up Honey Run. It was our family, and we couldn't do anything. I think it took us three and a half hours to get from Paradise to Chico. We went out toward Durham and went into North Chico. We had friends who had a garage there and a big parking area. We had asked if we could pull our trailer in, and that's where we stayed for the first night.

We ended up going to our daughter's in-laws, and that's where we spent the next five weeks. Going back to Paradise was just as hard. We had a surviving home, but we didn't know that. We just assumed the house had burned down. I remember when we left town thinking, please God, don't let it be hard on the bird and cat. It killed me thinking about them burning up. Maybe the cat was OK since it was outside. We kept driving to the shelter to see if they had the cat, and we saw a Town of Paradise truck parked at Chipotle and asked the man if we had our house. He didn't know. This man was very kind and said he would check for us. He did check, days later, and he told us, "By the grace of God, I have no idea why you have a house. And it looks like it has hardly been touched by the fire. You have a couple of broken windows and some of your yard is burned, but your house looks untouched. And you have absolutely no neighbors on your street. You only have one house at the end of the street, your house, and one at the dead end at the other end of the street. Everything else is gone."

Then he asked if we had an orange-and-white cat. That was our cat. The cat was in the yard. That was something. My poor cat. The man said, "Meet me in Chico when I get off work. If you give me your house key, I will have animal control come up and get your bird and your cat." So that's what we did. We gave him our key and made arrangements, and they came up and got in the house. The bird was fine. They had to find the cat.

The cat had been burned on all four of his paws. They took him to the shelter, and we got the call that the cat was there. By the time we got to Chico from Browns Valley, they had so many animals and so many injured animals they couldn't take care of our cat. They shipped the cat to the San Francisco SPCA. The bird was there. I do have to say that the SPCA was absolutely phenomenal for what they did for us and for everyone. They had to ship these pets to wherever they could find a place. They kept our cat until February because we couldn't take him back because of the cleanup we had—dirt, debris, ash—but they treated the cat for his burns. They kept him in the shelter, put him into a foster home, and drove him home from San Francisco. I can't thank them enough for their kindness.

We were in Browns Valley for five weeks because they wouldn't let us back into Paradise. Not many people had their homes. We were a small minority, and it is a very different group of people to be in. Yes, you go through all of the trauma, heartbreak, and everything else, but it is different. Here we were worried to death that someone was going to break into our home because it is still here, and people were doing that. They go to disaster areas, break into homes, and steal what they can steal. We were paranoid that was going to happen.

For us, this is our investment. We both retired, and we put our whole lives into our home. We have been there for forty-five years. The other thing that is very stressful and traumatizing for all of us is having a surviving home. Our neighbors do not. Our entire family has lost everything they own. Everyone in our family lost everything. We are happy to have a home, but you still have that survivor's guilt. It is very hard to deal with.

The first day we got back, we were watching neighbors coming in and digging through the ashes at their homes. Seeing neighbors and telling them I was so sorry our house didn't burn down. It is hard to put into words. Survivor's guilt is real.

It goes deeper than having a surviving home. It was harder to deal with the insurance company. It was just totally different. There's no help because we had a surviving home. We might have extended our resources, such as the bank account, just finding a place to live temporarily and buy food and all the other things. It was a whole new animal.

I feel fortunate we all made it out alive. All of us did—my husband's family, our daughter, but all of them lost their homes, and some of them lost two homes. We are happy we made it out because so many people did not make it out. In the same sense, it's something that will affect me the rest of my life. It will never go away. It is down to pre-fire or post-fire. There's always a feeling of, oh, I have that, no I don't, it burned in the fire. So even with a surviving home, there's still loss. Our storage shed had things that were irreplaceable, especially things that were my husband's and my father's. That is all gone. It is just difficult.

We are all going through this. There isn't a right way or a wrong way to grieve. We have to go through it however we have to go through it. I want to try to help people feel better, but I can't because they are in their own grief. I belong to a lot of the social media groups, and I see people who are doing better and people who are actually doing worse. It is really heartbreaking because there is nothing I can do to help them. It is just the stages they have to go through. Some people have died. Some people have ended their lives.

My husband's dad helped build the Welcome to Paradise signs. Charlie Todd was the one who designed the signs. Charlie was a building contractor in Paradise, and my husband's dad worked for him. Charlie is not around anymore, and I got ahold of his son in Salmon, Idaho to see if I could get some more information about the sign—he is actually a stepson of Charlie's. He couldn't provide me much information on the sign. My husband's family has lived here since the mid-1950s, so you know it is a good long time.

# Lucy's Reflections

### What was the worst part of that experience for you?

It is like one big snowball. There were so many things that were really bad. It was frightening for me realizing we needed to go, and we needed to go now. I didn't care if he got the trailer or not. It didn't matter. We just had to get out of there. That was scary. There is just so much, I can't really nail it down to one or two things.

### What would you have done differently?

I would have grabbed that little old lady and thrown her into my car. I would have hopefully thought we had room in the trailer, and I would have put my bird in the trailer in the birdcage. I didn't.

### How have the recent fires affected you?

It is a trigger. I saw the smoke; I was trying to find out what was wrong. The most difficult, frustrating thing for us is what happens when the power goes out. If you have Comcast, they don't have a generator, so you have cable and TV for only a few hours. If you don't have a smartphone or a tablet, you have absolutely no access to any information about what is going on. That to me is maddening.

Apparently, the town council is going to address that with Comcast. I am pretty supportive of the town. It hasn't been easy for them. We have been writing the playbook for disaster. Here we have a radio station that was disabled in the fire. This should have been one of the first things that could have been up and running. At least then we could get access to the news and information. Some people, of course, have no power and a lot of things don't work. Some of us were fortunate enough to put in a whole-house generator. We can run our whole house when the power is out, but our TV and internet don't work. If I didn't have an iPad, many times I wouldn't have had access to information.

The Bear Fire was scary. My son happens to work for the railroad, so he is in and out because of his job. He travels all over so he doesn't really have a home except for the trailer he takes with him to where he works. He happened to be here when the fires in September happened. He and my husband spent the entire day watering down the house and the yard, and all of the neighbors were doing the same thing. I was on the iPad trying to get as much information as I could. It is critical to get the radio station up and running.

### What did you learn from this experience?

I am a lot more forgiving of myself. I am pretty much a goal-oriented person. I make a plan, and I get it done. Part of it is realizing I am not the same person—the person who went to bed on November 7 and got up on November 8th. I am different. So, for me, I am more forgiving. If I don't feel like doing something, I don't worry about it. It will be good the next day, and that is usually not like me. I found that, at least for me, depression—there are still days that I get depressed— was triggered by the fire. I thought I would never be at a point where things I like to do didn't have much meaning to me anymore.

118

I think I am better, but I can remember sitting and thinking about sewing, and I didn't want to sew. For me, it was really hard. I had just retired from my job. I had been working since I was sixteen years old. So, I had one year of retirement, and I was having fun. I was gardening, sewing, and doing all the things I couldn't do when I was working a full-time job. Then this bombshell hit, and it changed everything. I am more forgiving of myself. I am tougher than I knew. I thought I couldn't survive anything like that, but I could.

Now, I can't take anything for granted anymore. I learned it is OK to have PTSD. It is OK to have those trigger moments. It is OK to grieve in whatever way I have to grieve. There is no right or wrong way to handle it.

### What are you still struggling with?

I think what I struggle with is the fact that my husband and I had a plan. He retired six years ago. The plan was that, when I retired, we would finish remodeling our house and pack our trailer and take off and travel and look for a new place to live. We loved Paradise, but we didn't love California. That was the goal—to find another place we would love to live, not in the state. We can't do that now. The house is not done, and there are other things to do. So, we are kind of stuck with the house.

### What keeps you going?

I have to keep going because if I stop, I will stop forever. My daughter and her daughters keep me going. I have three wonderful granddaughters and a new great-grandson. That's always important—family, and to keep plugging along every day. That's all I can do.

### *If you could give another survivor any advice, what would it be?*

Be patient with yourself. Be patient with others. Don't assume everyone is going through the same thing. I find it frustrating because people get upset at other survivors. "You should be doing OK." Just be patient and take it step by step. You will have good days, and you will have bad days. It will never leave us, but I am hoping, at some point, that it will be interwoven into your personality where you can deal with it. You can't ever forget it. We get to someplace where it doesn't affect us.

# Clinician's Corner Survivor's Guilt and Acceptance and Commitment Therapy

**W**e often hear the term "survivor's guilt." We will discuss what survivor's guilt is, the best way to deal with it, and how to heal from it. Survivor's guilt is the guilt a person feels from surviving a life-threatening trauma when other people may not have. The subconscious thought process behind survivor's guilt is essentially that they have done something wrong by surviving when others may have lost their homes, important belongings, or their lives. Survivor's guilt is a symptom of posttraumatic stress disorder and is often accompanied by other PTSD symptoms (Leonard, 2019). We will talk about these co-occurring symptoms in just a bit.

Lucy's story is one that not everyone can say they can relate to. Her home, her cat, and her bird were all safe and in relatively good condition. Lucy has a lot to be grateful for, but at the same time, the guilt she experiences from her home still standing is a normal and common feeling for fire survivors to have. While not everyone may experience guilt, there is a level of empathy that usually comes with knowing that other people may not have been so lucky. Survivor's guilt can result from multiple different types of experiences and include war veterans, 9/11 survivors, first responders, cancer survivors, organ transplant recipients, natural disaster survivors, those who lose a family member to suicide, and parents who outlive their child (Leonard, 2019). In a 2018 study of those attending a UK trauma clinic, nearly 40% of clients had experienced a trauma in which someone died. 90% of those reported guilt about survival, mostly at severe levels (Murray, H. et al).

Survivor's guilt is not limited to only living through a trauma when others have died. Another form of survivor's guilt a person can experience is guilt associated with what that person did or did not do during the traumatic event (Leonard, 2019). In Lucy's reflections, she mentions things she would have done differently. Lucy stated that she would have made room for the older woman she had passed on the road, and she would have put her beloved bird in the trailer to take with her. These are thoughts that can sit heavy on a person.

As we mentioned above, survivor's guilt is a symptom of PTSD. This means that in addition to feelings of guilt, a person can also experience flashbacks of the event, obsessive thoughts about the event, anger and irritability, a lack of motivation, problems sleeping, feeling the need to isolate, and thoughts of suicide (Leonard, 2019). If you struggle with any of these symptoms, please know you are not alone, and there are people who can help you. We want to empower you to reach out and get help. You do not have to struggle through on your own.

How does a person who is experiencing survivor's guilt and possibly associated PTSD symptoms heal and feel better? There are a few interventions that therapists use to help heal PTSD and survivor's guilt. One immediate symptom-relief technique is to practice mindfulness to ground yourself back into the present moment. Survivor's guilt has a lot of anchoring into the past, and "should have, would have, could have" thoughts can often lead to depression. Mindfulness, as we have discussed in other chapters, can help you gently come back to the present moment. It is in this present moment that symptom relief can be obtained.

Anxiety has a tendency to anchor our thoughts in the future, and depression has a tendency to anchor our thoughts in the past, neither of which currently exist. The only reality we have is in the present moment. To recap, mindfulness techniques include practices such as deep controlled breathing, meditating, aromatherapy, reading, and even drinking water slowly. All of these help your mind stay focused on the here and now.

Another important intervention is to connect with friends and family. While this may seem trivial or as if it would not help, it is a great way to again bring you back to the present moment with people who are thankful that you did survive. Sometimes we can lose the perspective of our purpose in our grief but connecting with friends and family who love us can remind us that we still have purpose in this life and that there are people who would miss us if we were not here. If you are struggling with survivor's guilt, please know that your life has meaning and purpose, and your story is not over. You are worthy of a life worth living.

A technique therapists might use with those who struggle with survivor's guilt is Acceptance and Commitment Therapy (ACT) developed by Steven Hayes in 1986. ACT helps with psychological flexibility and is a form of behavioral therapy that combines mindfulness skills with the practice of self-acceptance. When aiming to be more accepting of your thoughts and feelings, commitment plays a key role (Ackerman, C., 2017). Clients often try to avoid, deny, and repress these deeper emotions, which can then have a larger negative impact on them mentally, emotionally, and physically. Here, acceptance is key. Many of the emotional struggles that people deal with are because they are trying not to feel the negative emotions. In ACT, the most important part is to accept the feelings and commit to feeling them, processing them, and working through them.

As we can see from Lucy's story, part of her acceptance was forgiving herself. She has accepted where she is. Acceptance for where she lives, acceptance about how she feels, and acceptance for where she is in her healing process. Can you find forgiveness for yourself and where you are in your healing process? Here is a quick exercise to help you tap into self-forgiveness.

First, sit or lie down in a comfortable position. Close your eyes and take a few deep breaths in and out. Next, place your right hand on your chest over your heart, then place your left hand on top of your right hand. Continue to take deep breaths in and out. Notice the feeling of your hands moving up and down with the rhythm of your breathing.

As you focus on the movements of your breath work, you will say a series of statements aloud. Allow these statements to be absorbed into your emotional space. As you say these statements, have grace and patience for what you have experienced and where you are in your process. and if you are possibly still struggling with some aspects of your mental health. Remember, the goal is to find acceptance for yourself so you can then work toward change. Say the following statements to yourself:

- I love and accept myself for where I am at this very moment.

- I love and accept myself for what I have experienced.

- I love and accept myself even if I still struggle.

- I love and accept myself for doing the best I can right now.

- I love and accept myself for getting up in the morning.

- I love and accept myself for getting through my day.

- I love and accept myself just the way I am.

- I love and accept myself.

- I love and accept myself.

- I love and accept myself.

Congratulations! If you completed the exercise, you just took the first step in forgiving yourself and accepting yourself right in the here and now. Next, let's reflect on the exercise. If you are into journaling, jot down some thoughts you had about this exercise. If you are not much of the journaling type, that's OK. Mentally answer the following questions:

- What was it like to do this exercise?

- Did it feel forced or was it easy to do?

- Did you feel yourself finding acceptance or did you feel resistant?

- What thoughts or emotions came up for you as you did this exercise?

Please know that whatever you have experienced and wherever you are in your journey, you have the power within you to heal, and we're so glad you are here.

# KELLY'S STORY
# I'm Here: My Mom and My Stuff Are There

Agonizing helplessness set in while I watched from the Dutch Bros drive-up in Chico. What I saw looked like an apocalyptic cloud. My seventy-eight-year-old mother was up the hill. My stuff was up the hill, too—in Paradise.

Paradise was burning.

At about 7:30 a.m. on November 8, 2018, it was a normal day turned completely on its head. My mom called me while I was in line at Dutch Bros, and I was crying, and I was scared. The girl at Dutch Bros pretty much climbed out the window to give me a hug. I was so scared, and I couldn't do anything for my mom. There was no way I could get up there to help her. It would take my mom, her neighbor, and as many pets as they could fit about five hours to reach safety in Oroville, which normally takes thirty minutes.

My niece drove her boyfriend and me to Oroville to get my mother. My mother didn't want to live anymore. She had already been through another fire in 2008. It should have been a normal day. I had just taken my teen son to school. We noticed the "cloud" in the air above Paradise, and I thought this must be really bad. Everything happened so fast. It was a big black cloud.

We drove to the bottom of Skyway and thought it really didn't look good, and I guess I took my son to school. At the same time, my mother was trying to drive through fire to escape. I was on and off the phone with her. I just had to wait.

The traffic fleeing the fire was so intense. It was chaotic. When we met up with my mom in Oroville, I put her in the car, and we ended up at my sister-in-law's, in Chico. I don't remember much after that. There were other realizations and revelations that followed. It was super scary, and it didn't even hit me for a good while that all my stuff was up there. Three days before, I was moving out of an apartment in Chico and waiting for another apartment, so I had taken all my stuff up to my mom's, in Paradise, two or three days before the fire. I had some of my clothes, but everything else was at my mom's house.

My mom lost her home, and all my belongings were in my mom's home. Luckily, she had really good insurance, so she bought a trailer and put it on my sister-in -law's driveway, which was crazy, so that made me homeless, too.

The trauma of the day of the fire was not limited to that one day.

That's why these fires are so scary. We were scared to death, and my son was scared to death. The sky turned orange. I didn't realize how much this affected me. My mom went back down to Chico, and all the ash was falling.

# Kelly's Reflections

### What was the worst part of that experience for you?

The worst part of the experience for me was afterward. I did not know how to come out of it. I remember posting on Facebook that I don't know what to do. I don't know how to come out of this—I don't know.

My friend's cousin from high school, who lives in St. Louis and that I knew back in the day, wrote me a message: "This is what you're going to do. You're going to grab onto your kids, you're going to hold onto your kids, and you're going to be grateful you're alive, and you're going to tell your kids we are going to rise from this, and we are going to do it, and you're going to lean on God, and you're going to move forward."

### What keeps you going?

What keeps me going is my kids, whom I adore.

### If you could give another survivor any advice, what would it be?

If I could give another survivor any advice, I would say to be nice to yourself. Be understanding and forgiving of yourself. Trauma is the cause of so many things, and this is only one trauma. I've had trauma since I was five.

# Clinician's Corner
# Anxiety and Panic Attacks

Anxiety can be a common experience when a person goes through a scary event, such as Kelly did. Anxiety is a normal and instinctual response to certain circumstances. In fact, sometimes anxiety can be beneficial to our health and safety. Anxiety is our mind's safety mechanism, alerting us when there is danger and helping us prepare to fight or flee. According to the Anxiety & Depression Association of America (2021), also referred to as ADAA, anxiety disorders are the most common mental health issue in the United States. Anxiety disorders affect close to 20 percent of the population in a given year. This is roughly around forty million adults in the US.

According to Psychiatry.org (2021), anxiety and anxiety-related disorders are a response to the anticipation of a future worry or concern. So, in essence, there is a fear about a future-focused person, place, thing, or event. Kelly experienced anxiety not knowing where her mother was or if she was safe. For many of you, like Kelly, the unknown may be a scary place. Surviving a trauma, such as a fire, can definitely provoke a lot of fear and anxiety about what the future holds and whether or not you would be prepared the next time. We hope there is not a next time, but those types of thoughts are often accompanied by anxiety, your body's feelings, and your mind's perception of not being safe. Again, anxiety is a normal human experience. It develops into a disorder when the level of anxiety becomes debilitating to a person's daily functioning.

Let's talk about how anxiety presents and a few of the different types of anxiety-related disorders that are common within a clinical context. As you read through the anxiety symptoms checklist below, feel free to mark them off and rate them from 1 to 5, with 1 being rarely experienced and 5 being often experienced. This will give you an idea of how significant your experiences may be. Anxiety can feel different to each person, but the symptoms experienced are typically similar across the board. According to the Mayo Clinic (2018), common anxiety symptoms are as follows:

- Feelings of tension or restlessness
- Sense of danger, panic, or doom
- Rapid breathing
- Sweating
- Trembling
- Increased heart rate
- Trouble sleeping
- Feeling weak or tired
- Difficulty controlling worry
- Experiencing gastrointestinal (GI) problems
- Trouble concentrating
- Avoiding things that trigger anxiety

An Anxiety Symptoms Checklist you can use to assess your level of anxiety can be found on the resources page here:

www.SiftingThroughTheAshesResources.com

**Here are some of the various types of anxiety disorders that clinicians often see (Mayo Clinic, 2018).**

*Agoraphobia* is an anxiety disorder that is characterized by a fear and avoidance of places or situations that cause panic due to feelings of being trapped, helpless, or embarrassed.

*Generalized anxiety disorder* is characterized by persistent and excessive worry about activities and events, even daily or routine issues. The requirement for this disorder is that the worry is out of proportion to the actual circumstances, is difficult to control, and affects how you feel. This is often experienced along with other anxiety disorders or depression.

*Separation anxiety disorder* is usually experienced in childhood and is characterized by anxiety that is excessive for the child's developmental level and is related to the separation from parents or caretakers.

*Social anxiety disorder* is characterized by high levels of fear, worry, and avoidance of social situations and feelings of embarrassment, self-consciousness, and concerns about being judged or viewed negatively by others.

*Specific phobia* is a disorder that is characterized by high levels of anxiety or panic when exposed to a specific object or situation and a high desire to avoid it. Phobias can provoke panic attacks in some people.

**Here is more information about panic attacks:**

*Panic disorder* involves repeated episodes of a sudden and intense feeling of fear or terror that reaches a peak within a short amount of time. To have panic disorder, a person must have experienced a panic attack. One main characteristic of panic disorder is an intense fear of experiencing repeated panic attacks. Essentially, the fear of having a panic attack can precipitate a panic attack. Other symptoms of panic disorder are shortness of breath, chest pain, heart palpitations, hot flashes and sweating, trembling, dizziness, numbness, nausea, and a sense of impending doom (Mayo Clinic, 2018). Many sufferers of panic attacks have described feelings of impending death due to the intensity of their physical sensations during the panic attack. This is not meant to scare you. It is meant to reassure you that the feelings from a panic attack will subside, and you will be OK, even if it does not feel that way.

To reduce the symptoms of anxiety, and more specifically, panic attacks, the following practices are recommended for you to try. If you are experiencing panic attacks, you should also reach out to your physician to rule out any physical reasons for your anxiety and panic attacks.

One symptom-reducing technique is deep breathing, which has been discussed in previous sections. It is such a valuable intervention. Deep breathing, or box breathing, can not only help you slow your breath, but can also activate your body's natural calming function. You will want to take a deep, slow inhalation for four seconds, hold your breath with your lungs full for four seconds, slowly exhale for four seconds, and hold your lungs empty for four seconds (Cleveland Clinic, 2021). Continue to breathe in and out in this rhythm for two to three minutes. You should start feeling calmer and at ease.

Another symptom-reducing recommendation is Rock Mindfulness. This exercise not only brings you back to the present moment, it also allows your thoughts to be focused on something else, which can help reduce anxiety and the thoughts associated with panic attacks. Step-by-step instructions on the Rock Mindfulness Technique, as well as other anxiety reduction exercises, can be found on the resources page here: www.SiftingThroughTheAshesResources.com

# BETH'S STORY
## The Trees

On November 8, 2018, our lives as we knew them changed forever. I woke up that morning to have my coffee around 6:30 a.m. and turned on the TV. Scrolling on the bottom of the screen was an emergency notice of a fire in Pulga. I called my neighbor because I knew his wife sleeps in. My neighbor told me he was packing up in case we had to evacuate. He alerted his wife, who said that Pulga was fifteen miles away and we had nothing to worry about, that we would be fine.

Since we had previously experienced the 2008 Humboldt Fire, I decided to walk down our driveway and look around. My other neighbor said, "Good morning, Beth, what's up?"

I told him, "There's a fire!" and pointed to the smoke in the sky above his roof. Nothing was said after that, and I guess we both went into survival mode.

I then went back to the house and woke up my husband. I told him there was a fire and we had to go, NOW!

We had important papers, jewelry, medications, etc. handy every fire season, but this wasn't fire season, it was November. In a panic, my husband couldn't get our cat out from under the bed. She sensed our panic and fear. I told him to flip the mattress. He did, and we trapped her and got her in her carrier. I grabbed some framed pictures, yanked quilted wall hangings I had made off the walls, and clothes that were handy, and we loaded up both of our cars.

I looked out our front window and saw my neighbors drive through another neighbor's property to get to another road instead of using Skyway. We didn't think to do the same at the time, but we later found out it wasn't any better as far as gridlock. Our neighbors were directed to Bille Park for a while, until they were told they had to leave due to the fire approaching.

My husband led the way as we both drove off from our home. I took a picture of our home, thinking it may be the last, and I sobbed as I drove off. I was really scared!

At the end of our street is Skyway, and it was still gridlocked! We attempted to leave several times, each time hoping it would get better, but that didn't happen. At one point, a truck was letting us in, onto Skyway. My husband just sat there in a daze. I had to get out of my car and tell my husband, "Go! He's letting us in!" Traffic was still not moving.

A motorcycle driver, in a panic, hit my side mirror. He was driving between vehicles. We sat in traffic for what seemed an eternity. We still weren't moving.

I got out of my car again and told my husband, "I don't care if I have to drive my new car in the ditch, we are getting off Skyway!" He led the way. As we drove in the ditch to turn on Montna, I received a call from our neighbor who lives below our property on the canyon, which is also accessible from Montna, to come to her house. When we got there, she wasn't there, but her husband was blowing leaves and pine needles off their roof. Suddenly, someone frantically hollered, "Fire!"

My husband and our neighbor went to try to help. There were spot fires everywhere, and they did their best to put them out. My neighbor's wife returned and she and I went inside to check if our zone was called to evacuate; it wasn't. It seemed every zone number was called to evacuate but ours. My husband walked up to our house and hooked up a fire hose to a 550-gallon water tank we had and started spraying water down toward the canyon. The winds were increasing, and I hollered at my husband, "The roof!" He couldn't hear me because of the winds. He had previously told me the water would only last about five minutes. He sprayed the roof and went around to our back patio and sprayed down what he could.

He also turned the sprinklers on for the front lawn. Our yard was cleared to the dirt as it has been for all the years we have lived in Paradise, eighteen years at the time. No leaves or weeds on the ground. As far as defensible space, we were good.

My husband and I walked back down to our neighbor's, on the canyon below our house. I received a call from the previous owners, who were our neighbors for sixteen years and had moved to Alaska. They were concerned for our safety. During our call, the winds increased even more, so I said I would call back when I could and told them, "We love you!" We had also previously discussed, on the phone with my cousin, a retired firefighter, finding somewhere to shelter in place. There was a well next door. My neighbor and my husband went to check it out. They were concerned about the small space and limited oxygen. My husband knew how claustrophobic I am and that I would panic.

My neighbor and I went out in her yard and there were more spot fires. I turned their water hose on and discovered the hose had melted.

The four of us stood outside my neighbor's garage and put on masks that they had, because of the heavy smoke. The winds continued to increase. Then my neighbor asked, "What's that noise?"

I told her, "Propane tanks are exploding!" Due to the winds, the sound of them exploding seemed muffled.

As we looked up the canyon, we saw pine trees go up like torches. That's when we knew we had to leave. We jumped in all four of our vehicles and drove toward Skyway, once again only to find gridlock. We stopped at the corner of Skyway and Montna, and a woman was shouting, "Don't take Wagstaff! It's on fire!" It was only one block down from where we were. I kept thinking this can't be happening.

At the house on the corner of Montna, a woman was watering down her yard. We got out of our vehicles and talked about what we should do. We noticed two free-standing swimming pools and thought about jumping in them to shelter in place, but that wasn't feasible for us with our cat. We ended up parking and abandoning our cars on Skyway, leaving everything in our vehicles. So much for being prepared. The sky was turning darker.

We walked down Skyway at a pace faster than the cars were moving. My neighbor traded off with my husband carrying our cat. I pointed to the sky, which was orange and eerie, and asked my husband, "Is this it? Is this Armageddon? Are we going to die?" He didn't respond. I held his hand as we walked toward Wagstaff. The trees were burning on the corner.

We got separated from our neighbor, and I kept yelling his name and looking back, hoping he would catch up with us. We found out later he was helping to get another neighbor to safety. We walked about a mile and a half to Holiday Market. On the way, we noticed a stucco building with metal roofs and a fire engine in the lot and said, "Let's go there!" We crossed the street and went to the parking lot. My husband sat with our cat, against the building, trying to stay out of the smoke. There was also a woman on a horse, trying to keep him calm.

Suddenly the sky turned dark as night!

My neighbor approached a firefighter and asked him if we were safe there. The firefighter said they were trying to get cars off Skyway and get Holiday Market opened—I assumed to shelter in place. Neither one happened.

A friend called me from Livermore, a town 175 miles away, to check on us. We didn't realize the fire was all over the news and didn't know the severity of it at that time. We just knew we had to get out of Paradise to safety.

We finally reconnected with our neighbor, who was frantic because he had no way of knowing we had crossed the street and gone to the Holiday Market parking lot. We tried calling him on his cell, but it kept going straight to voicemail. Later, when we texted him, he told us he didn't realize where the Holiday Market was.

He finally found us, upset due to the fear of being separated. It was difficult for all of us to comprehend what was happening. There appeared to be fire everywhere. Unbelievable. We were all scared for our lives. I think I remember hearing someone hollering we had to go and go now!

We all jumped in my neighbor's friend's car and put our cat in the trunk, trying again to leave Paradise via Skyway. As we were leaving the Holiday Market parking lot, the trees behind the Jack in the Box across Skyway ignited into flames!

It's difficult to remember what was said between us, but we all knew we were in immediate danger.

Traffic was still moving slowly down Skyway. We approached Neal Road, and I could hear someone screaming. I rolled down the window and heard someone yelling, "Not that way!" He directed us to turn on Neal Road. As we turned on Neal Road, there was a car burning on the side of the road. Both sides of the road were on fire! We could feel the heat inside the car, and I was afraid the car would catch fire. We continued toward Highway 99.

Suddenly we were in a blanket of smoke, and our driver shouted, "I can't see!" All we could see were two taillights in front of us. Still not being able to see anything but the taillights, our neighbor's friend asked us, "Should I follow them?"

Sitting behind her, I said, "What choice do we have? Go!"

We were all silent. I don't know how many miles it is from Skyway down Neal Road to Highway 99, but it seemed to take forever. I didn't think we were going to make it. We continued to drive, and the sky started to clear as we approached Highway 99. We all cheered, "We made it!" and thanked God!

The woman who drove us out had nerves of steel and kept her cool the whole time. God bless her; she saved us! Later, we discovered that Neal Road burned all the way to Highway 99 and jumped the freeway. God was guiding us and our driver. We had made it out alive.

We turned north on Highway 99, traffic still at a crawl, and we ended up on the Midway in Chico, which took hours. Periodically, when traffic stopped, my husband got out to check on our cat; she was still in the trunk.

Our driver said she was going to the Kmart parking lot to connect with her father, then she drove us to a friend's home in Chico. Of course, we could not thank her enough.

Later that evening, we learned from the news that where we were staying was now under an evacuation warning. I started crying and said, "No! I can't go through this again!"

We eventually learned that our house was still standing, and our vehicles made it through the fire, even though everything burned around them. A friend sent us pictures of our house, and we saw drone footage on the news that showed our vehicles. It was hard to believe since the news stated that Paradise was wiped completely off the map! That was difficult to hear. It was a whirlwind of trying to figure out how to go about everyday life. We could not concentrate.

We had no vehicles, no clothes, no medications, or everyday necessities. We found ourselves to be short-tempered, and nothing seemed to register when we tried to carry on a conversation and decide what to do next. Costco in Chico ended up being a meeting place for Camp Fire survivors. We went to get some clothes there, and large flakes of ash were falling from the sky like snow. Cars were covered with the ash, and the ash was flying through the door into Costco.

When others asked if our house had made it, I would reluctantly say yes. My heart ached for those who had lost lives, their homes, their history. At times, I chose not to say our house made it. I was later told I was suffering from survivor's guilt.

We ended up staying at several places—four, to be exact—before moving back home to Paradise in February 2019.

Early on, we had friends in Oroville open their home to us and try to guide us on what to do next. We were in shock. We are so blessed to have friends and family help us through this unimaginable and devastating time. My girlfriend pleaded with me for months to seek counseling.

The last place we stayed was as far away as Oakland Hills in the Bay Area. We were advised not to move back home until the lots were cleared around our house, because it was toxic. We couldn't wait that long because of looters, and we worried daily. The lots around our home weren't completely cleared of debris until May 2019. I wish we could have waited before returning home.

Witnessing our neighborhood being scooped up into dump trucks created more trauma for me. I cried as I walked down the street, visualizing my neighbors' homes and what they had lost.

Paradise was in lockdown until December 15, 2018. There were a few exceptions. The National Guard was called in to protect what was left of our town and keep people out. It was difficult to hear that the town we loved and lived in for eighteen years had been destroyed.

We chose not to return home until the next day since we had fought to get out during the fire. I didn't want to sit in traffic to get back into Paradise! Since the Camp Fire, I find it difficult to drive in traffic and get triggered if another car gets too close or tailgates.

As we drove into Paradise, we were in disbelief. Paradise looked like a war zone! I cried as we drove up Skyway through town. Burnt buildings and cars lined the street. The trees and landscape were totally changed, gone. We tried to recognize our street. The street sign had burned. I don't remember what was said between my husband and me. We were in shock, once again. When we turned on our street, everything was gone— every home except for ours and one other. The canyon next to our house and the trees lining our property all burned. Sadly, our neighbor's home was gone.

Unfortunately, I had friendships lost or strained due to the Camp Fire. Some friends were lost through misunderstanding and others were not as supportive as I would have hoped for. But I also gained new friendships. Some are Camp Fire survivors and others showed kindness and the willingness to listen to anything I had to say. Some others think we should get over this and move forward. We will never forget and get over what happened that day. We just have to learn how to deal with it and to move forward.

Paradise as we knew it is gone. It is still hard for me to accept that to this day. Our small town was nestled in a forest, no fences needed for privacy. Our trees were our privacy. That has all changed. I have also cried over the loss of our trees, as they were cut down around our home. They will never grow back to their former grandeur. Not in our lifetime.

We still hear the sounds of chainsaws to this day. The quietness of Paradise is also lost for years to come. I am still angry and in disbelief. The destruction of our town, Paradise, could have been prevented.

## *Trees*

*By Joyce Kilmer*

*I think that I shall never see*
*A poem as lovely as a tree,*

*A tree whose hungry mouth is prest*
*Against the earth's sweet flowing breast;*

*A tree that looks at God all day,*
*And lifts her leafy arms to pray;*

*A tree that may in summer wear*
*A nest of robins in her hair;*

*Upon whose bosom snow has lain;*
*Who intimately lives with rain,*

*Poems are made by fools like me,*
*But only God can make a tree.*

# Beth's Reflections

### What keeps you going?

My husband's love, his understanding and emotional support. And for putting up with my anger and the emotional roller-coaster ride dealing with me from the aftermath of the Camp Fire. And for being patient and letting me find my way. Our cat, Maggie, she knows when I am down and comforts me and makes me laugh.

The continued love and support of family and friends. My new friends, some who experienced the Camp Fire and know what I went through and others I met through counseling and therapy.

Our neighbors who returned. Our new neighbors, who still see the beauty in Paradise, chose to still live here. Having neighbors around us again is comforting to me. I feel safer. After the Camp Fire, we had one other house on our street that survived besides ours.

Watching wildlife return. We had thirty hummingbirds the first spring. Deer, bears, foxes, skunks, squirrels, coyotes, and so on. Watching our garden grow back, except for the weeds, of course.

Watching the fifteen redwoods my husband planted grow to twice their size!

### Whom do you resonate with since the fire?

Thoughtful, kind, loving, and caring people. And those who show empathy and try to understand what we went through escaping the Camp Fire. Someone early on after the Camp Fire gave me a pin that said, "Kindness Matters," and we became friends.

As I met people in town, I ran into those whose houses also survived. We were told we were the lucky ones, even though living in what they now refer to as the Burn Scar hasn't been easy and has its challenges.

### What are you grateful for?

I am grateful that we survived the Camp Fire when eighty-five lives perished. And that God guided us through.

I am grateful for my husband's love, support, and endless patience with me. Patience is a virtue.

I am grateful for family and friends.

Our cat, who comforts me when she knows I am upset.

We are grateful that our house survived, even though at times I am told I suffer from survivor's guilt. There were times when people asked, and I didn't want to say our house made it.

I felt sincere empathy for those who had lost generations of homes, photographs, and heirlooms that can never be replaced. Grandparents, parents, aunts, uncles, sisters and brothers, everything gone. They must all feel an unimaginable loss.

I am grateful for Heartstrings, a counseling service that helped me learn the tools to deal with the trauma, triggers, and PTSD caused by the Camp Fire.

**What has been the worst part of this for you?**

Driving through fire, thinking we were going to die. Witnessing our town being destroyed and later knowing people died. Losing friendships due to misunderstandings as a result of the Camp Fire. Mentally not being able to concentrate and do things I could normally do.

**What are some of the residual thoughts about the Camp Fire?**

It could have been prevented. How we drove through fire feeling the heat on the car, thinking we could have burned alive. The lives lost and our town destroyed.

**What, if anything, would you have done differently?**

Nothing. We survived!

**What did you learn from the experience?**

How much my husband loves me and wants to protect me. That I am stronger than I realized. I learned that family and friends are important and not to take them for granted. I learned that love and kindness will help you through any experience.

**What are the long-term effects of the fire for you?**

Trauma, PTSD, and survivor's guilt. My anger toward PG&E. If they maintained their equipment, lives wouldn't have been lost and the town of Paradise would still be here. I miss our trees throughout the Ridge. Fear of another fire. In the summers of 2020 and 2021, we were under evacuation warnings.

I told my husband I can't keep going through this. The small town of Greenville was destroyed by the Dixie Fire in 2021. I was triggered by the smoke and threat of the winds shifting and the possibility of the fire heading our way.

Trying to find some form of normalcy and moving forward. Letting go of things I can't change, as a result of the Camp Fire.

# Clinician's Corner
# Anger

In Beth's reflection, there is a level of anger toward the fire and PG&E, in Beth's words, not maintaining the equipment. Anger is often a large part of the trauma response survivors experience when processing their emotions. Anger is a core piece of the puzzle that bridges the gap between the initial event and overcoming the event. According to Davis (2022), anger serves the purpose of alerting us we are in some distress. Although anger is uncomfortable mentally and physically, it motivates us to address our needs, desires, and threats. However, unprocessed anger leads to many problems. When anger or rage is expressed appropriately, the survivor of trauma feels relief, and their bodies and minds have a chance to heal. Anger is also a common response to events that seem unfair or in which you have been made a victim. Anger is a survival mechanism. It shifts the mind's focus from victim to survivor.

Anger can also be seen as our "inner system's" attempt to feel heard, seen, and justified, especially if we feel that something was done to us. We know we experienced something horrible, and we know it was not right, so our anger is there to protect us and to say, this is not right. Beth expressed her anger toward the fire and the responsibility of PG&E to maintain their equipment. Her "system" sees the injustice, and her anger is that inner part of her saying, this is not right; this is not fair.

Anger is an automatic response of posttraumatic stress disorder (PTSD) and can lead to greater difficulties in life if it is not processed in a healthy manner. Unprocessed anger can lead to emotional outbursts, aggressive behaviors, relationship conflict, substance use or abuse, and even physiological manifestation in your body. According to the US Department of Veteran Affairs (2021), those who experience PTSD may consistently feel on edge or be irritable and easily provoked. This level of functioning can lead to seeking out situations that require you to be alert to ward off danger. Instead of changing the inner dynamic to ease the PTSD, the PTSD causes the person to subconsciously seek an external environment to match their feeling of hypervigilance. The US Department of Veteran Affairs also states that the other end of the spectrum is the use of alcohol and drugs to reduce the level of inner tension. Keep in mind that this is also a spectrum, and that some people may be somewhere in between the two extremes.

Posttraumatic anger can be broken down into three significant aspects. These factors can lead a person with PTSD to react in anger, even far beyond the initial threat to their safety.

- *Arousal* is when the anger is marked by physiological reactions in the body. This is when the trauma centers of the brain have been activated for whatever reason and alert the body to a potential danger in the environment. Organs such as the heart, circulation system, glands, and the brain kick in and prepare the body for fight or flight.

- *Behavior* is when the anger is channeled into unhealthy action. This behavior is a coping mechanism that proved to be a form of protection at the time of the trauma, though it may not be necessary once the threat has passed. These actions may look like aggressiveness, impulsiveness, being consistently late, or poor job performance at work. On the other end is self-blame, which can result in substance use or abuse and self-harm or self-injury.

- *Thoughts and beliefs* are when the anger is stuck in the mindset of a person with PTSD. The initial traumatic experience can sometimes "plant a seed" of thought that gets "stuck" and results in a hypervigilance of repeated thoughts. The thoughts experienced are that the threat is consistent and is perceived to be ongoing.

We have explored what anger is and how it can present itself in your experience. Let's discuss how to heal your anger and what you can do in your life right now to better cope with the feelings that may or may not come up for you on a daily basis. We first want to validate your feelings and your experience. As you have read above, anger is a normal part of processing a traumatic event. If you are feeling anger, or any other negative emotion, please know that you are safe. What you are feeling is part of the healing process.

According to Substance Abuse and Mental Health Services Administration, anger can negatively affect your health by way of increased blood pressure, rapid heart rate, short and shallow breaths, and tightened muscles. Relaxation and mindfulness are suggested as useful interventions to lower your overall stress and help manage your anger in productive and healthy ways. Practices such as deep breathing will allow your lungs to become fully expanded with air, thus enabling your body's natural calming capabilities. As previously discussed, box breathing can be beneficial to balance the emotional regulatory system. In box breathing, you will want to inhale for four seconds, hold your breath with your lungs full for four seconds, exhale for four seconds, and hold your breath with your lungs empty for four seconds. Try to repeat this cycle for two to three minutes.

Another relaxation practice is visualization; specifically, creating a safe space in your mind that you can travel back to when you are feeling like your anger is becoming unmanageable. Practice this right now. Read through the prompts and then try it for yourself.

Close your eyes and take three to four deep breaths. Settle into your seat and allow your body to relax. In your mind, go back to a place and time where you felt most at peace—physically, mentally, and emotionally. This could be the ocean or a cabin in the woods or any place and time where you were truly at peace. As you go to this place in your mind, notice any sights, smells, or sensations you feel as you visualize yourself there. As you spend more time in this safe space, notice how your body feels. Can you feel yourself relaxing yet? If not, you may need a few more minutes in this space. If this space increases your anxiety, stress, or anger, then this may not have been a time when you felt most at peace. Try to find another space and repeat the exercise.

Another common relaxation exercise developed by Dr. Edmund Jacobson in the 1920s is called Progressive Muscle Relaxation (PMR). This method of relaxation involves alternately tensing and relaxing 14 different muscle groups. According to the U.S. Department of Veterans Affairs (Mirgain, S. PhD and Singles, J. PsyD, 2016), PMR is a two-step relaxation practice to reduce stress and build awareness of sensations of tension and deep relaxation in various muscle groups. The first step in this practice is to create tension in specific muscle groups and begin to notice what tension feels like in this body part. The second step is to then release this muscle tension and begin to notice what a relaxed muscle feels like as the tension drains away. By moving through the body, alternately tensing and relaxing different muscle groups in a certain order, one builds awareness of how to recognize and differentiate between the associated feelings of a tensed muscle and a completely relaxed one.

Often, it is recommended to create tension and relaxation several times in the same muscle groups, with diminishing degrees of tension, to deepen awareness and train the body to more deeply relax. Through repetitive practice, a person can then induce physical muscular relaxation at the first signs of the tension that accompanies stress. After the practice, there may be one or two areas that are still tense, requiring one to repeat tensing and relaxing that muscle group. This is done by starting at the top and moving down your body, tightening and relaxing the various muscle groups. By "over-tightening" your muscles and then relaxing them, you can release the tension that had built up by the anger you held in your body. You can find a Progressive Muscle Relaxation exercise on our resources page here: www.SiftingThroughTheAshesResources.com

Gentle stretching or yoga is also a great relaxation technique. These can be great ways to channel and release the stress in your body. As you move your anger out of your body, you can start to feel calmer and more in control of your emotions.

Communication is also key to managing and coping with anger. The use of "I" statements can allow you to articulate your feelings without placing blame on other people, places, or things. These statements can sound like this: I feel frustrated that the dishes haven't been done.

Also, try to avoid using the words "never," "always," and "should." These words are rarely true and are projective in placing blame. This can make the other person feel defensive and less open to finding productive solutions.

These are just a few ways to encourage you to learn to manage and better cope with your feelings of anger. Remember to have patience and grace with yourself as you navigate your healing journey. The magic of healing is in the journey, not the destination. Take your time, progress slowly with intention, and allow the experience to shape you and help you grow. You can find the Anger and Irritability Symptoms Checklist on the resources page here:

www.SiftingThroughTheAshesResources.com

# BRIANNA'S STORY
# Guilt and Residual Pain

It started as a day like any other day. My husband, Chad, and I lived in a cottage apartment in Paradise. We got up kind of like we do every morning at 6:30 or 7. He made coffee, and I got ready for my day and ate some breakfast.

My friend and I texted back and forth. She lives in Chico and took a picture of the smoke in Chico because it looked like somebody had started a fire down there. I was curious and opened my blinds. I sent a picture to her, and I wrote, "Actually, it looks like it is closer to here."

I always go with my gut feeling. It's a weird intuition I have when something doesn't feel right. Chad and I grew up with wildfires. We are used to the fires. I told him to pull the pictures off the walls because this fire didn't feel right. He kind of argued with me, but I convinced him to get them off the walls.

When I left for work that morning, the ash falling on my car was huge. That worried me, but I shrugged it off and went to work. Clients were in the office already. I was a lead staff of a day program for supportive in-home and day programs for people with disabilities. It was fulfilling and a hard job some days. Chad worked for the same company doing the business side of stuff. He didn't have to go into work until 9 a.m. so he stayed home. The clients already had the police scanner on, and they started to panic. I told them to turn it off to avoid panic.

Within moments, we found out the fire was at Ponderosa Elementary School, and they were evacuating houses over there. I called Chad and asked him to start getting the pictures in the car. Something didn't feel right. I needed the pictures out of the house. He didn't listen to me and said, "No, Brianna, it's fine," so we hung up the phone. I was frustrated. Another call came in minutes later saying the high school was being evacuated. Then we were evacuated. I called Chad again and said, "I need you to go," and his response was, "I'm not even dressed yet." I didn't give two shits if he was in his underwear. He needed to get out of the house.

We got all the clients packed up and then we got another phone call. I could hear, in the background, the sheriffs on their bullhorns yelling, "Get out!" I headed to my house and called my dad, who lives in Montana, and left a message telling him we were fine, just being evacuated. I made it sound like it wasn't a big deal because I didn't want him to panic.

I then called my mom. Most of the time she says she can't talk right now and she's at work. I remember mumbling, "Pick up the fucking phone, pick up the fucking phone!" and when she did, I didn't even give her a chance to talk. I just spouted off that we were being evacuated. She stayed on the phone with me pretty much through the whole thing. I got to the house, and my mom said, "Grab this, grab that, and grab your important paperwork."

I got in the house and Chad already had quite a bit of stuff in his car, pictures included. We grabbed my jewelry. We'd been married not even a month. We didn't take many of our wedding gifts—they all burned—and I didn't get my wedding dress. I know a part of it was that I was hoping I would come home, and it would still be hanging in my closet.

My mom mentioned the big screen TV Chad had recently bought. I told Chad to grab the TV. He said he was not worried about the TV, and I said, "Yes, you are. You still owe money on the damn thing." When he grabbed the TV, I grabbed the Xbox, cords, and a couple of games and shoved it all in the car. I was running out of the house with our marriage license in hand yelling, "Ha-ha! You can't trade me in now." Our neighbors were laughing pretty hard.

Before I got off the phone with my mom, I asked her to call my twin sister. We have this weird twin thing; when something is wrong the other one knows. My sister lives in Susanville and recently had a baby. She was struggling with some postpartum stuff, and I didn't want her to worry. I told my mom, "I don't care what you have to do. You lie to her and tell her we are in Chico and we're fine." My sister called when we were escaping. I lied my ass off. I said we were down in Chico, and everything was fine, and we were fine. She didn't know I lied until a month later.

When we were leaving the apartment, I was staring at everything. I thought I was going to die without this stuff. Chad actually yelled at me. It was the only time he used his military voice with me. We had a fire about a hundred yards behind our apartment. I knew when we left, we weren't coming back.

We were stuck on Elliot Road for a couple of hours. Before we left, we decided if the fire overtook the cars, we would ditch the cars because the stuff wasn't worth it. I was on the phone with Chad. I told him it was midnight black. He said, "But there is blue sky in front of us." And he said, "Brianna, what's most important is what's in front of me right now." That actually put a lot in perspective for me.

We finally got on Clark and the gas station across from us was on fire. I was really hoping it wouldn't blow up because it was right next to a propane tank. An old woman in front of me was trying to turn around because she left her purse at home. A gentleman on a motorcycle noticed. I put the nose of my Jeep in front of the woman because I didn't want her turning around. I did my best to make sure she didn't. The motorcyclist pulled up next to us and asked her what she was doing. She said she left her purse at home and needed to get gas. He pulled out his wallet and gave her forty bucks and told her, "I don't care what you need to do. You're not turning around. Just go, get gas in Chico—just go." I kept her in front of me the whole time.

When we got from Clark to Pentz Roads onto Skyway, there was a man standing there trying to direct traffic. He didn't realize he stepped into my lane so I couldn't turn and got upset with me because I was not turning or moving. He slammed his fists on the hood of my car to tell me to move. A sheriff's deputy came up and grabbed him and pulled him out of the way, saying, "Dude, you're in her way," and I went past him.

I was on the phone with my mother. The clinic on Skyway was burning. I had clients who lived by the clinic. I told my mom, "It's burning, oh my God, it's burning." The people I cared about—their homes were gone! I told my mom I was going to have to drive through the fire and I was terrified. I watched two people in a Honda Civic ditch their car. I couldn't get them in my car, I didn't have room, but the truck behind me jumped in front of me and let them in. The driver opened the door and they jumped in.

I drove through the flames. I kept my cool pretty much throughout the whole thing. Everyone else was driving around like idiots, and I was asking my mom on the phone, "Why are they being idiots?" But I just about lost my cool when my mom asked, "What's that sound?" as I was driving through the fire.

That was enough to knock me back into, "Are you kidding me?"

She asked, "Are you serious?"

I said, "Yeah."

She could hear it, but it sounded on her end like I was right up against a campfire; that's what it sounded like. I pushed through it. I got out and I saw blue sky and I said, "Oh, my God, Mom, it's the sun."

Chad was behind me. That was the other hard part, not knowing where he was. While talking to him as he was going through the fire, I could hear the stress in his voice, which didn't help me. When he told me he got through it, I hit the gas. I was doing 90 mph down Skyway to get out of there.

All the workers agreed to meet at Kmart, our emergency place to meet. I met up with my boss, coworkers, and clients. I cried because I had two more clients behind me, and we didn't know where they were. We couldn't get ahold of the workers who were with them. The owners of our company and their three sons were still behind us. When they got down there, we all hugged and cried. A couple of staff left their clients and me at the end. We were all there for twenty or thirty minutes. One of the clients didn't have staff to go with him. We got hotel rooms in Red Bluff, and I jumped in and I worked—I worked the rest of my day.

That night, Chad and I got the last hotel room in Corning. We stayed one night. We went to Round Table Pizza because I used to work there. I needed a sense of normalcy. I needed people I knew around me. We ate there, and I only had a couple bites. Then we went to the hotel. The next morning, I knew I was miscarrying—I had found out, a couple of days prior, that I was pregnant, and I hadn't had a chance to tell my husband or anyone—nobody knew. I felt like he was already holding me up as it was. He had to hold himself up and hold himself together. I couldn't throw something else on him.

I went back to work that next morning. The other owner of my company lectured me about how I needed to pull myself together to be there for the clients. I finally got the guts to tell her I was miscarrying. The fact that I was even at work should have been enough for her. Chad and I worked sixteen-hour days with the guys in the hotel. He was never trained how to work with the clients but was very quickly trained then. My day-program boss stayed in the hotel with the guys, so if a staff member didn't show up, she worked that shift. She didn't get to go home. She had her two girls with her, both of whom were in high school, and they helped with clients.

I was in shock and didn't know what to do. My mom told me not to make major decisions when I was emotional. But when I got to the hotel room and looked at Chad, I said, "We're done. We're gone. I want to go to Montana."

He said, "No." But I was working so much to the point where I was mean to the staff. If a staff member

160

from Chico called in sick because they were tired and it was too rough to work with the clients, I asked, "Did you lose a house? Did a member of your family lose a house?" When they said they didn't, I said, "Then I don't give two shits about how tired you are. You need to come into work." I threw myself into work and into my clients because they lost just as much as we did.

We went back up to Paradise the day they opened it—I was working so much I needed to go—and that was even harder. I got to where our apartment used to be and cried. Soon after, we ended up getting an apartment; we got lucky when so many others didn't. A friend brought us furniture from her old apartment, and she went shopping for us to have kitchen supplies. We still don't know how to thank her for helping us. I was broken because the only thing from my papa I grabbed was his golf trophy. The stuff that actually meant something is hard, but I am less materialistic now.

# Brianna's Reflections

### Where are you now? How are you now?

We moved to Montana where I do adult case management for work.

We are doing well. We don't know if we will ever be fully OK.

### When did you decide to move?

Chad decided we were moving to Montana in January 2019. There were tears of guilt and relief. I knew I had reached my limit. The next day, I met my boss, and I put my two-week notice in, and I apologized. I said we need to go, and we need to do this. It was hard leaving her because she had such a big heart.

### What do you miss about Paradise?

I had a habit of locking the door and not taking my keys out of the door. The keys would stay in the door all night. I've never lived in a place that was safe before where you could leave your keys in the door and no one would bother you. That is what I miss the most—the safety of Paradise. Most people in Paradise were welcoming. I used to work with clients with disabilities and the severely developmentally delayed. After the fire, I worked with one client quite a bit. When I had my miscarriage just after the fire, I was working with him. I loved his laughter. He would laugh about any little thing.

### What are some of your feelings looking back?

I was numb, and then I threw myself into work. I didn't feel it was fair to wallow. I didn't get a break from work until I broke. It was just before Christmas when I came home after another sixteen-hour shift. I got home from my hour drive and just dropped and told my husband, "I need you to tell me what to do because I can't do this anymore."

### What was your support system like?

We got really lucky with the support we had. I feel guilty sharing my story. I know there were so many people who didn't have that support, but I still want to share mine.

We are super thankful for the support we had; we wouldn't be where we are without it. When my boss found out her home was saved, she didn't want to tell me. I said, "No, I am happy. I don't want anybody to ever lose a home."

### What was it like returning to Paradise after the fire?

Christmas day after the fire was the last time I went up to where my apartment was. Recently, when we went up, we didn't go by where our apartment was because I wasn't ready for that. Being able to go up and see how much growth there is actually helped me a lot.

### What has helped during your recovery journey?

What's been helpful getting through some of this is watching some of the documentaries and knowing what other people went through. I know my story isn't as bad as some other people's. Part of me feels guilty that it's not as bad, but the other part makes me feel grateful for that. It's helped me to kind of move forward from it. I have an attitude of a glass half full rather than half empty. I wanted to see Paradise and the growth after the fire. It helped.

# Clinician's Corner
# Relationships and Isolation

Trauma can have a significantly negative impact on relationships. During a traumatic event, a person gets emotionally pushed, prodded, and stretched to their max. Each person experiences, copes with, and manages stress and trauma in their own way. The difficulties come when a relationship experiences a Big T Trauma, because each person in the partnership is not only going through their own struggles, but now they also have to work through the struggles of the relationship. In the case of Brianna and her husband, Chad, they evacuated as a couple and survived the Camp Fire. There are multiple layers to their story: each of their personal individual traumas and their trauma as a couple.

Trauma changes the way we interact with and relate to others. It challenges our safety and security in our world. These uncertainties can and will affect how we relate to our loved ones. Survivors often feel vulnerable and unsure what is safe in their world. This level of anxiety can create a destabilization for the relationship (International Society for Traumatic Stress Studies, 2016). Symptoms of PTSD include irritability, aggression, dysregulated mood, flashbacks, and loss of control in life. This can be hard on the friends and family of a survivor. The problem is compounded when both people in a relationship are struggling with PTSD and each is in their own bubble of processing.

Partners can also become frustrated with one another because of their difference in processing. Perhaps one person is a talker and the other is an avoider. Maybe one person weeps to express their pain and the other person represses their pain. There are so many variables that can affect each person and add to the entity of the relationship. It is important for couples to allow each other to process in the way it is best for them (Pollock , 2014).

There is a tendency to want to fix or prematurely heal the partner relationship. This can result in increased frustration, additional pain and triggering, and possible resentment of the other person not understanding what their partner is going through. Pollock (2014) says that the best course of action is to just be available to listen to your partner and simply validate their emotions. Phrases like "that sounds really difficult to deal with" or "I can imagine this is really hard for you" are validating statements that let your partner know you hear them, see them, and are there for them.

It is also important not to make any assumptions about your partner's process and not to take it personally if they are struggling. Many couples report that their partner seems to have changed in the way they communicate, show affection, or how they just show up. Trauma does change people, inside and out. So, if you find that your partner is isolating and is not as communicative as they once were, have patience with them. Processing deeply heavy emotional trauma can be a long and dark journey that is sometimes impossible to articulate. Be the loving, supportive light to guide them home when they are ready.

If you are the partner who is struggling with PTSD or just not feeling like yourself, this is normal. You are still on the grief/healing path. Communicate your needs to your partner in the best way you can and seek professional mental health support to help process your experience. Involving your partner in your healing process can help them feel more included in your new world as a survivor. This, in turn, can make the relationship stronger and more resilient in its survival. Couples who come together and support each other in healthy ways tend to come out the other side of trauma stronger. We want to give you the tools to learn healthy coping techniques as a couple. You can find a Couples Coping Checklist on the resources page here:

www.SiftingThroughTheAshesResources.com

Partner isolation is common in relationships that have undergone trauma. The feeling of needing to separate oneself from others is a form of self-preservation (Foy, 2019). Self-isolation can also be a reflection of the internal emotions of the person suffering with PTSD. They may feel alone or that no one understands them. Foy says that by isolating, survivors can avoid having to explain their complex emotions to others, especially when the survivor may not even know how to articulate their feelings. They feel it is easier to be alone than to talk about feelings that are not completely understood in the first place. When a loved one reaches out to survivors who may be self-isolating, Foy also suggests it can have adverse effects. The survivor can sometimes perceive the "reaching out" as an attempt to change the behavior.

If you have a loved one who is isolating, allow them the space and time to process their trauma in their own way. Let them know you are there and will be available to support them when/if they are ready. Then take a step back to allow that space. This can be hard for loved ones. The first instinct is to move closer, but this can feel pushy, overwhelming, and create even more pulling away by the survivor.

If you are the self-isolator, we want to tell you that we see you, we hear you, and we are here for you when you are ready. Reaching out for help can be hard. You have to be ready for the help. You need to be ready to talk about and deal with the emotions behind your need to isolate. You are encouraged to seek professional mental health assistance if you feel yourself experiencing any of these symptoms:

- Suicidality

- Depression

- Impairment in your daily functioning

- Intrusive thoughts

- Nightmares or disturbing dreams

- Substance use due to your trauma

- Any other behavior that you find troubling

We hope this information helps you and your loved one understand how trauma can affect a relationship. It is not just the individual who is challenged in a traumatic event; the relationship, as a separate entity, is also tested. It has its own level of PTSD. The most important thing to know about this is that the trauma happened to your relationship. Externalizing the problem can help you and your partner see yourselves on the same team. What you have survived together is also what will allow you to thrive together. Please seek help, communicate, and be open about how you are feeling. Your relationship is worth it.

# ANNE'S STORY
## No More "Safe Place"

I'm a single woman. I celebrated my sixtieth birthday about seven months prior to the fire. I lived a quiet life. I enjoyed painting, gardening, quilting, and jewelry design incorporating rocks and beads.

On November 8, 2018, the Northern California Camp Fire ravaged my hometown and surrounding communities, destroying everything in its path. The devastation included my home in Old Magalia, taking with it its entire contents, five generations of memories, keepsakes, thousands of pictures, and my livelihood as an artist, which supplemented my social security income. Additionally, it devastated my lifelong goal of owning my own home, without debt, and the life I had dreamed of living near family and friends.

My grandson, Joseph, the most important focus in my life, lost his "safe place." Joseph is a beautiful, sweet, autistic, nonverbal, musically inclined, intelligent child. He was three years old at the time of the fire. He had lived with me four days and nights a week since he was ten months old. A special needs therapist commuted to my home four days a week to work with Joseph on speech and sign language. Joseph was making incredible progress and recognized it himself. He began making eye contact and signing; knew his colors, the alphabet, and numbers; and he surpassed expectations by using words verbally. He was out of diapers and could brush his teeth. He was proud of himself and was a happy child.

Joseph had his own bedroom with a race-car bed, Lego table, musical instruments, puzzles, and a learning tablet specifically designed for autistic children. The walls were decorated with the baseball caps my father had collected for over twenty years. The caps were given to me after my father's passing, and I cherished them. Autistic children do not adjust well with change. Losing my home meant Joseph lost his home also, and he lost his safe place with me.

On the morning of November 18, I woke in the throes of a kidney stone attack. I had an appointment for pre-operative testing to determine further treatment at Oroville Hospital later that morning. I never made it to that appointment.

The morning had an eerie feel I would describe as unusually quiet and still, an orange-yellowish soft glow on the horizon through the trees to the east of my property. There was no breeze or sound of birds. The deer family, normally meandering through the yard at that time of the morning, was absent. It was then that I noticed the large plume of dark smoke rising from the far east side of Sawmill Peak Lookout, and it appeared to be intensifying in size and ferocity.

I sent a text to my next-door neighbor to confirm her cable and internet were down, as were mine. Unable to get any news channel, I tried calling 911, but there was no answer. I immediately called the Magalia Fire Station. I asked if there was a fire and if Old Magalia would need to evacuate. The frantic male voice said, "Fire in Concow," and "Probably." The sound of phone lines ringing in the background made it impossible to hear if he said anything further before the call dropped.

With a sense of urgency, I woke my tenant, John, who was living on my property in his fifth wheel. We assessed the situation and agreed the direction of smoke seemed to be moving south, toward Table Mountain and Lake Oroville. The skies directly above us were blue and clear. The winds were calm. There was no smell of smoke.

Only weeks before, I received an Evacuation Instruction Notice in the mail. I tacked it on the back of the door exiting the house. We read it and, following its instruction, John drove us three blocks to the designated meeting place for Zone 7, Magalia Community Church on Old Skyway. The notice indicated fire officials would be available there to advise us on evacuation and routes and protocol in the case of a fire.

We were two of a handful of other neighbors. There were no officials from Butte County, CAL FIRE, CHP, the Department of Forestry, fire departments, Magalia Sheriff Department, Paradise Police, etc. I took a picture of Sawmill Peak Lookout. The plume, much larger but still on the east side of the Ridge, was moving south. I spoke briefly with a neighbor I had never known, then turned my attention back toward the lookout. With cell phone in hand, I snapped a picture. The image I captured was the source of terror and disbelief. The large plume of smoke on the other side of Sawmill Peak, blowing in the direction of Table Mountain, had changed direction. It had traveled over the Ridge, down the canyon, crossed the West Branch Feather River, and was heading directly toward us with a vengeance.

John and I were standing alone in the parking lot of the church. I was paralyzed with fear. The same people

I was speaking with only moments before were running for their vehicles and screaming. Their screams were directed at John and me. They were telling us to run, to get into our vehicles—to leave now. The skies grew dark and black. The blue sky directly above us changed to a dark black/gray. The wind was blowing from every direction, and there was a deafening sound as the fire blazed directly toward us.

We ran for John's truck and knew we had to evacuate immediately. We drove back to the house where I grabbed the small dog, Rex, that I was taking care of for friends while they were vacationing. I grabbed a cell phone charger, a pillow and blanket, and evacuated wearing the clothes I would wear for the next two weeks. John was rushing to try and load some tools he needed for work in the back of his truck. I remembered that the Evacuation Instruction Notice had advised us to open electric garage doors and drive cars out, in the event of a fire, before PG&E cut power. I tossed my key ring to John from the deck overlooking the driveway and garage, and he rushed to pull my car out as the garage door was rising. The power went out at that time, leaving only inches of clearance for my car to pass through.

I realized I had not seen my next-door neighbors, who had three special needs children and a fourth child due in a few weeks. I called and told them of the fire. Within minutes, they were loading their children and a few items in their car. We exchanged well wishes, quick hugs, and said our goodbyes. I remember the surreal feeling that I might never see them again, as they pulled out of the driveway. The children, who called me "OG," for Other Grandma, were crying and waving out the back window.

John and I talked briefly about which way to evacuate. He wanted to go downhill, taking Skyway to Chico.

It was a shorter drive under normal circumstances, but I speculated that the traffic was already jammed. We knew the town of Paradise was already burning, and the Safeway shopping center was already gone, through calls we were getting from out-of-town friends watching the news. Feather River Hospital was threatened. The whole town and surrounding communities were under mandatory evacuation orders.

My father taught me the different escape routes from Upper Skyway—routes from DeSabla, Stirling City, and Inskip—when I was a teenager learning to drive. He instilled in me the necessity to know how to drive on dirt and rough mountain roads. "You should always have a backup plan on how to get out of a situation safely, especially if it's a fire," he had told me. He spent a lot of time teaching me those back roads, a manual transmission, and when to use four-wheel drive. Forty-four years later I was in a position to decide on a backup plan. I felt confident, yet terrified, about taking the rough back roads, but we had no time to consider another option. I drove down my driveway, Rex and Tako, John's small dog, in the passenger seat, with John following close behind me in his truck.

John's truck was very low on gasoline and needed to be fueled before we could get off-road, so we decided we would stop at a small market/gas station three miles up from where we were. We were about a half mile from the house, approaching the intersection of Skyway and Old Skyway. The traffic coming down the hill was congested, the traffic light was out, and the cars were unwilling to let anyone into the lane to turn right down the hill. I motioned that I was turning left, to go up, along with the truck behind me. They let us through, and we headed uphill.

My cell phone rang. A good friend was calling to make sure we were getting out, NOW. He got a call from someone close to my neighborhood reporting that the flames were approaching fast. I assured Sam we were safe, for the moment, and heading in his direction, up Skyway. He, his expecting wife, and two boys ages one and three, needed help loading their cars.

We stopped at the gas station. I drove to the back parking lot and waited for John to get the twenty-dollar limit allowed, per person, of gasoline. The four lanes to the pump were backed up about a quarter mile down the road. There was chaos everywhere and tensions were high with most everyone. I witnessed fighting, crying, screaming, animals howling, cars running into each other. Everyone had only one mission to accomplish that morning: get out with family, pets, cars, and whatever they had time to pack into the car before leaving their homes, jobs, schools, appointments. Nothing seemed real.

Leaving the gas station, we went up Skyway, turning right onto Steiffer Road. We were met by Sam in the driveway, frantic, trying to get his young boys, wife, and a few necessities packed up, and get out. We helped them get on the road and again waved goodbye to a much-loved young family with a new baby on the way. Not knowing if I would see them again, I turned away. I ran back to my vehicle, prepared myself to lead the way through the back roads, and prayed that these two special families would find their way to safety and hold their newborn daughters in a few weeks.

I knew we had to escape and do it fast. The fast-moving fire was being driven by high winds that seemed, again, to be coming from every direction at once. The skies were becoming darker with every moment. The smell of smoke was thick. The fire itself sounded evil and wicked-like, howling with deeper sounds of growling. I remember thinking, it's alive, and it wants to kill all of us.

That is when my mom called, frantic. She saw on the morning news channel that Paradise and surrounding communities were on mandatory evacuation due to a fire and wanted to make sure I was aware of the orders. I talked with her briefly, trying to reassure her I would be safe. I told her John would be following me, going up to the back roads to evacuate the way Papa had shown me. I told her how much I loved her, not to worry, and we would talk soon. She was saying the same to me. I knew that neither of us were convinced when the cell service towers went down and the call was dropped.

As John and I were leaving Sam's house, John realized that his close friend, Pam, was home alone without a vehicle. In poor health, she would need help getting out of Magalia. She lived only a mile from where we were, down Skyway, the opposite direction of our intended escape route. We discussed a plan where John would head down, with a quick pickup and turnaround. I would wait for his return, and we would continue up Skyway to the dirt roads and evacuate. We agreed, and he left.

Rapidly, those plans went wrong. Within minutes, a man wearing a uniform came to my vehicle window and instructed me to "get moving." I was parked to the side of the residential street, out of any traffic. I tried to explain that I would only be there a few minutes waiting for my traveling companion and would then caravan uphill. He remained adamant that I move on and turn left, going downhill. He said unless I was getting in line for gas, I could not turn right and go uphill, against traffic that was coming down.

I was terrified about John and me being separated, and I feared he would turn back downhill if he was unable to find me waiting for him where we had agreed. The officer left me no other option except to surrender to his orders. I turned left, merged into slow traffic, and began the descent downhill, into chaos and life-changing events.

As hard as I tried to stay focused and maintain an optimistic attitude, I knew in the deepest part of my being that this was a bad situation, a true emergency, and life-or-death decisions were necessary immediately, with only one directive. My father's words. He was very deliberate in what he taught me about the risks of a fire, and the absolute, only option to escape without delay was to evacuate uphill, on dirt roads.

I knew I had to turn around and go back. Cars, trucks, RVs, vehicles pulling travel trailers or boats or utility trailers were backed up in the small streets and main roads. There were people on motorcycles, off-road quads, and bicycles. There were people running while pushing a wheelchair or gurney. There were young parents running with a stroller while balancing a toddler on their hip. There were men on horses while leading more horses tied to a rope. I saw a pregnant woman on horseback holding a very small child seated in front of her.

I continued in stop-and-go traffic downhill, entering Paradise limits. The roads feeding onto Skyway were creating a traffic-bottleneck situation, barely moving or not at all. I saw familiar and unfamiliar faces. They were frantic and crying. There were vehicles on fire, people inside screaming for help, and it was too hot to approach close enough to open the doors to free them. Dogs in the beds of trucks, on fire from burning embers the size of salad plates falling from the sky. I witnessed events no one should see. These things will haunt me until I die.

Human instinct to survive overtook me, and without hesitation I made a sharp left U-turn and was going uphill again. Drivers who were still maneuvering their way downhill were eager to allow me to make the turnaround, one less car in front of them and their evacuation. I was eager to find a safe place and starting to panic about finding John. I headed back uphill, trying desperately to erase the images I'd witnessed. Without a cell phone signal, John and I were unable to contact each other.

John returned to Steiffer Road, where he last saw me, and when I wasn't there, he also began to panic. Remembering how determined I was to evacuate on the back roads, he found a safe place to pull to the side of the road, free of heavy traffic, and waited until he saw me approach. I saw his truck and pulled over. After a quick exchange of our feelings, fears, and frustrations, we headed down a long, dirty, dusty, rough, washboard switchback, four-wheel-drive mountain road, hoping to find safety in a burning hell. John followed close behind me.

It took hours to finally reach a paved road. We were met by CHP and CAL FIRE uniforms. They were placing orange cones and tape barriers across the entrance to the paved road. They wanted to know if anyone was following behind us, as they were preparing for a rescue mission if needed. We were unaware of anyone else, and they instructed us to head west on the paved road toward Chico and shelter.

I was able to find a radio station in the car that was reporting that the Neighborhood Church, on Notre Dame Boulevard in Chico, was housing fire victims, and to go directly there. John and I pulled over and decided this would be our plan. Unfortunately, we were unable to get to that shelter. All roads leading there were closed, allowing vehicles still evacuating the fire to be a priority. Detours for the closed roads led us in the opposite direction. It was during one of those detours that we found the East Avenue Church setting up for evacuees. They opened their doors to provide shelter. For those of us who were fortunate enough to escape the inferno, it was our only "home." It would be my refuge for the following seven weeks.

Hours later I was still alone, in my car, in a dry dusty field behind that shelter. I remember thinking everything looked blurry again. I caught my reflection in the rearview mirror. My face was blackened with dirt and smoke and streaked with dried tears. I wondered if my tears blurred my vision. That day is a nightmarish blur yet very clear in my memories. I was one of the fortunate evacuees.

I had confirmation that my home and its entire contents were gone the following day, unlike most of the other evacuees at the shelter. They wandered around aimlessly, sobbing, asking each newcomer if they had any information regarding their neighborhood. Or worse, had they seen a family member—holding out a picture, trembling, fighting back more tears. The scene resembled a refugee camp as makeshift tents, knapsacks, sleeping bags, and rolled up blankets became a safe place. I was hungry, cold, scared, lost, and I was alone.

Sleep eluded me as I watched the horizon continue to glow orange at night, and the blackened skies on smoky days made it almost impossible to breathe. As hard as I tried, I couldn't escape the images of people and pets burning in their cars. I was surrounded by the sound of screams, children crying, dogs howling, swearing, and prayers. All of that, and more, echo in my head. The smells still remain unfamiliar to me, yet all too familiar. Images embedded in my brain. Images no one should see.

The recall of the evacuation might seem melodramatic to some. I assure those people, unless they were there, experiencing what it is like to run for your life, with only minutes to decide which direction to escape, that it is unimaginable. There was no warning. No alerts were issued on my cell phone; there was no knock on the door. There were no officials at intersections directing traffic or at designated meeting places with instructions.

There was no time to pack my computer, laptop, external hard drive, and dozens of thumb drives. Multiple tubs with five generations of photographs, marriage licenses, death certificates, love letters from World War II, wedding dresses, jewelry, and coins were lost. I was the keeper of our family history—the safe place. When I drove away from my home on November 8, 2018, I wanted to believe the family history would be spared, like the times before when I was evacuated. I remember praying that I would return home, grateful for the false alarm. I was terribly mistaken.

The Camp Fire engulfed my town, my home, my memories, my livelihood, and my dreams for Joseph. It took our friends, family, pets, and physical and mental health. And it did not fall short in destroying the lives of children and men and women of all ages.

To this day, it still feels surreal. When I wake, since the fire, I force myself to not open my eyes for a few minutes. I listen, smell the air, and try to imagine that none of it happened. I tell myself, when I open my eyes, I will be in my own home, waking up on the antique iron and brass bed I've had since early childhood. Joseph will be sleeping in the next bedroom, dreaming sweet dreams.

It's been a long year. I've done everything I can in an attempt to move forward. I sought to find a place to call home. I have spent this last year completely displaced. First, the shelter, where the norovirus outbreak forced a lot of evacuees into their cars, including me. After living in my car, I was "blessed" with a FEMA trailer. It was at the Orland Fairgrounds' overflow parking lot for the livestock stables in Glenn County. The second night I was there, a stabbing took place, leaving one man with a slashed throat and the assailant at large. I spent my nights there, isolated. I spent my days traveling one hour to my property in Magalia, digging and sifting through the ashes. I would arrive on my property at sunrise and work until after dark, using the headlights of my vehicle as my light source. This was a distraction for me—looking for anything from my past that I could resurrect and treasure.

Finally, I was able to find a fifth-wheel RV I could purchase. It was pulled to Camp DeSabla through funds available from Butte County. The FEMA camps were closing, and that was the only option available. I dry-camped there without electricity or running water. The fifth wheel had a built-in generator that I was able to run on propane in order to have lights, hot water, and charge my cell phone. The cost for propane was a minimum of $25 per day. It cost approximately $750 a month in propane, far exceeding all the utility costs in my home combined. Cell phone signals are weak in DeSabla. It was necessary to drive a few miles down the road to make calls or have internet service in order to stay in contact with my family and arrange to keep the progress going on my property with the county, utilities, permit applications, etc.

I have worked diligently, every day, trying to co-ordinate everything necessary to move the RV to my property. I wanted to go home. Dead and compromised trees had to be cut down and removed at my expense. I dug until I uncovered my septic tank and was able to get a temporary permit for a hookup to the RV. I paid to have a water test and meter with Del Oro, and I was able to run a water line from the public road to my flag lot and install a spigot. With a hose, I had water but was unable to drink it or use it to cook. I acquired a permit for a power pole. I had an electrician position a temporary power pole and panel to accommodate two RVs: one for me and one to help another survivor and friend, John, who was also wanting to go "home." This, too, required a housing permit.

Since doing everything required of me to go home, the county has established, as of December 31, 2020, that property owners can no longer live in a RV on their own property. Prior to the fire, my homeowner's insurance company canceled my policy after years of in-suring the home. I was told it was "a high-fire-risk" and they would not insure it. As an uninsured homeowner, without any funds to rebuild, living on SSI, I will, again, be homeless.

Physically, I have suffered with numerous con-ditions, namely arthritis in my hands combined with carpal tunnel and trigger finger. I have a lot of sleep-less nights because of pain and aching numbness. I have back and sciatica pain, undoubtedly caused by the months of clearing my property—the hard work of shoveling, moving trees, and building retaining walls to prevent erosion.

I have limited finances and did a lot of the work myself. Most everyone I know was in the same position with their own property and no time to help. I'm now very limited in what I can do. I have shortness of breath with any exertion. This is a condition unfamiliar to me, as a runner and cyclist prior to the fire. My fingernails and toenails have a condition that has caused the nails to become misshapen and loose. I've had hair loss, gingival recession and weight loss.

Something became broken inside of me on November 8, 2018. As I write this narrative, twenty-two months after the fire, sleep still eludes me. The fear of the recurring nightmares is overwhelming. The visions embedded in my mind of people engulfed in flames in their vehicles, looking at me for help. I couldn't get close enough because of the heat. I watched them melt. I remember hearing screaming; I realized it was my own screams.

I ask myself, when I close my eyes and try to sleep, could I have done more? Did I try hard enough? I know I will never be the same person I was before the fire. Prior to the fire I was content, and I felt comfortable and safe. I was close to my family and enjoyed our holidays, mostly at my home. Every holiday or family get-together was cataloged and immortalized with thousands of pictures, videos, and tape recordings. How do I put a price on my entire life's photos and those of my great-grandparents, grandparents, mom, and now-deceased father, my children, and grandchildren, one who has passed away?

I had childhood friends that I communicated with on a regular basis. We reminisced about growing up and talking about having a family of our own, and later shared stories of our grandchildren. I had thousands of pictures from childhood: birthdays, Halloween, Christmas, Girl Scouts, school. On my seventh birthday, in

1965, I was given a Kodak Brownie camera that had been mom's. Until November 8, 2018, I had that camera, most every picture I had taken with it, and all the negatives. My best friend since first grade and I would sit for hours reminiscing over those pictures. Again, how do I put a price on something that is priceless and can never be replaced?

There have been long bouts of depression, hopelessness, and defeat since the fire. Not conditions I ever struggled with prior to the fire. The desire, and necessity, to return to my property kept me moving forward with a goal, and I was able to suppress the depression enough to accomplish that goal, to get Joseph back in my life, and me in his.

The most devastating loss for me has been the loss of time with Joseph. He has regressed in everything we had accomplished with the therapist. He's back in diapers, nonverbal, does not use sign language or have an interest in music. I am unable to have him with me, as before—four days and four nights a week. The drastic change in living arrangements without a room, toys, and everything familiar to create his "safe place" is not conducive to making progress for an autistic child.

The fire not only took away my most valued time with Joseph, it also took his progress and security away from him. He was an innocent three-and-a half-year-old boy. I have been able to see him seven times in twenty-two months, for about thirty minutes each visit. How do I get that time back? I can't. How do I put a price on that loss? How is it possible for him to understand what happened? Why I'm not in his life? He must wonder why he was abandoned by the only person he could depend on. Why can't he go "home" to his beautiful bedroom with his finger-painted train set and his painted footprints across the hardwood floor from when he took his first steps.

Knowing I will be homeless again in a few short months adds to the feeling of despair. I will have a RV, in need of repairs, and nowhere to go. I have been seeing a therapist since funding became available through a nonprofit organization. I suffer from memory loss and have a hard time staying focused. I've heard other Camp Fire evacuees refer to this as "fire brain." Forgetfulness is a common complaint. PTSD has had its effects as well. I'm unable to light a barbecue or propane gas oven without a panicky feeling of impending fire, explosion, or major disaster. I have anxiety whenever I see or smell smoke. I have looked to the east, from my property, toward Sawmill Peak, and mistaken clouds for smoke, at which times it was hard to breathe, and I felt the need to run, and escape.

I am not a writer. I am an artist. I paint mostly. This narrative is my attempt to paint a picture, with words, of the life I loved and lost in Magalia, California. My sentence structure may seem broken, or fractured, and may not flow smoothly. However, that, in itself, describes what life has been since that fateful day, November 8, 2018.

Recalling these events that changed my life forever, and everything that has transpired since, has been the hardest task I've ever had to face. Trying to make any plans for the future seems useless today. Where does hope come from? I am now sixty-two years old, with health concerns I didn't have before November 8, 2018. I live in a RV, on a piece of property that has only gravel, without any trees, plants, or flowers. I can't use the water to cook or drink. I have no fence for security as a single woman. I have nowhere to paint. I have no tools to make jewelry, or a place to work.

My hope is that my story, like thousands of others in our town and surrounding communities, will be heard. It is a story that should never have been necessary to tell. It didn't have to be this way.

# Anne's Reflections

### What was the worst part of the experience?

Having to make that left-hand turn and go down-hill and see the frantic chaos and all the other things I witnessed.

### If you could have done anything differently, what would you have done?

Evacuation. I don't know if I could have done any-thing differently. I would have picked up my hard drive (not set it down) with all my pictures and my "to-go" box would have had a few more things in it in preparation for leaving the driveway. I would have been more pre-pared than I was. The evacuation itself, there is nothing I could have done differently.

### What have you learned about yourself?

Oh, gosh, I am a lot tougher than I realized. I can do things that I didn't think I could do. I am strong enough and not that old. I still got it. I have learned that you can set your mind (like a goal). My one-year anniversary goal was to be back on the property. Not on the property in a tent, but I was trying to go home and I did it. I did not know I could. No one said, Anne, you can do it. You can do it. No one was pushing me to do it. Except I know I was, for me. And I can be more stubborn. One of the things I learned, is you don't always have to take no for an answer. Going back to when you were a toddler and asking, why, why, why? I learned you don't have to take no for an answer, and I am a lot tougher than I look.

Patience. I think about what I learned about myself. It is easy to say that everyone puts their pants on the same way, and everyone is no different from anyone else, we are no better than anyone else. What I learned is, we are much more equal than I imagined.

In that shelter, standing between people with dirty little kids. Maybe she was on drugs with no teeth and no education by the way she talked. On the other side of me was a woman, and a man in a suit and tie. He was a businessman who left a bank to get his wife out. They were not much older than me. Just like me, everyone had the same white face with ash. We were all standing there not knowing anything and we were all homeless. It dawned on me that everything this woman owned fit in a shoe box and this man probably had a house with a pool. We were all standing there—we had all lost everything. That's what I learned the most. I try very hard not to do it, to be judgmental. I have learned a lot about people and learned amazing things about how people can come together. With my first-generation family, I have a huge family.

**What are you still struggling with?**

Nightmares.

**What keeps you going?**

Tomorrow. I am not done on the property. I got the RV, and they did extend the date from 12/31/2020 to 12/31/2021. When I start feeling stuck, I tell myself, I am a banana. I think I survived. One of my exercises is to look at images of small cabins, to look at floor plans. My goal is to focus on my goals. I don't want a prefab house. I want it built. It doesn't have to be large, but I would like to have a single-car garage to put my car into. I am not setting my goals out of reach. I am optimistic. I want a cute fence to provide security and privacy. I planted tree seedlings. That's what I do to keep my focus on the future.

### If you could give another survivor any advice, what would it be?

If you want to go home, and this was your home, don't give up, don't give up. You can do it. You can do it, and if you can't, call me and we can do it!

# Clinician's Corner
# Posttraumatic Stress Disorder
# (PTSD) and Brainspotting
# Therapy

**L**ike Anne's story and many other stories, *Sifting through the Ashes* is about trauma. Trauma can look and feel different to each person. Some people experience what clinicians call Big "T" trauma. Big "T" trauma is the type of trauma that includes life-threatening and body-threatening experiences. These types of trauma are extraordinary and significant events that leave the individual feeling powerless and possessing little control in their environment. It is also the type of trauma that is associated with posttraumatic stress disorder (PTSD). Examples of Big "T" trauma are events that include natural disasters, terrorist attacks, sexual assaults, combat, car or plane accidents, etc. (Barbash, 2017).

Little "t" traumas are events that exceed our capacity to cope and cause a disruption in emotional functioning. These distressing events are not inherently life or bodily-integrity threatening, but perhaps better described as ego-threatening due to the individual left feeling notable helplessness. Little "t" trauma includes non-life-threatening events such as interpersonal conflict, infidelity, divorce, legal trouble, bullying, harassment, or loss of a significant relationship. While these events may produce significant mental and emotional damage, they are classified separately from those traumatic events that are considered life-threatening. This book is focused around the Big "T" trauma of surviving the Camp Fire of 2018 and how life-threatening trauma has an impact on a person's mind, body, and soul.

Surviving a fire like the Camp Fire is absolutely a Big "T" trauma. As a result, many survivors are struggling with what clinicians term PTSD, or posttraumatic stress disorder. The criteria for PTSD are extensive. It is important to fully understand, and face head-on, the things you struggle with. To help you understand yourself and what you may be still struggling with, you can find a Trauma Reactions, Emotions, and Thoughts Checklist as well as other useful tools on the resources page here:

www.SiftingThroughTheAshesResources.com

For a clinical diagnosis of PTSD, there are eight areas of criteria one must meet. Each area has multiple symptoms that may be experienced, and a person must have at least one of the symptoms in each criterion. The Diagnostic and Statistical Manual of Mental Disorders, Fifth Edition, 2013, outlines the eight criteria as follows:

A. Trauma Exposure (one required)

B. Re-experiencing symptoms (one required)

C. Avoidance behaviors (one required)

D. Cognitive distortion (two required)

E. Increased arousal (two required)

F. Duration (required) - *more than 1 month*

G. Functional impairment (required) - *symptoms create distress or functional impairment*

H. Exclusion (required) - *symptoms not caused by medication, substance use, or other illness*

Connecting with a therapist who is competent in trauma work can provide a comprehensive assessment and help you understand the level at which you may be experiencing PTSD symptoms. Here is a breakdown of symptoms to help you understand the residue of your traumatic experience.

We want to preface this next section by urging you to seek out a clinical mental health professional who can observe and assess your specific symptoms and therapeutic needs.

PTSD symptoms include recurring unwanted memories, upsetting dreams or nightmares, avoidance of thinking or talking about the event or places that remind you of the event, hopelessness, lack of interest in things you once enjoyed, feeling emotionally numb, difficulty making decisions, always being on guard, trouble concentrating, overwhelming guilt and shame, irritability, and angry outbursts. These are just a small selection of the symptoms that a trauma-informed mental health professional can help with. As stated before, a clinical assessment must be made for a diagnosis of PTSD. This diagnosis is important for insurance purposes. It is also important for the types of programs you may be eligible for. To see what is available for you, we urge you to seek professional mental health assistance.

One technique clinicians may use to guide their clients is to turn the traumatic memory from a visualization in color, as our minds typically see it, into a black-and-white visualization (Fuller, 2021). Now imagine that you are watching this black-and-white visualization on a movie screen. This practice lessens the mind's attachment to the event and moves you from being an actor in the movie to being an observer of the movie (in your mind). By seeing (with your mind's eye) your trauma memory as a black-and-white movie playing out on a screen in front of you, your mind is essentially tricked into disconnecting from the actual events. This allows you, the observer, to experience a decrease of PTSD symptoms.

Color is information waves of light that our minds pick up and take in. If we remove the Technicolor from the image in our minds, our brains connect to a different perception of information (Fuller, 2021). Since most of us see in color, being able to visualize in black and white helps us perceive the images as "not real." As with projecting the visualizations on a screen in front of you (again, in your mind's eye), this allows you to step out of the story line and watch it from a safe distance. When things start to feel too real, remove yourself from it and observe it from a movie-theater distance.

Brainspotting is an up-and-coming technique in the world of trauma therapy that has been gaining momentum since its development. Brainspotting was born from Eye Movement Desensitization and Reprocessing (EMDR). EMDR was developed by Francine Shapiro in 1987 and Brainspotting was developed by David Grand in 2003. Both brainspotting and EMDR use eye positioning and your visual field, along with bilateral stimulation, to access your subconscious mind. This allows for deep healing in a gentle way to help your mind process the thoughts, memories, and emotions of your trauma.

Brainspotting is a therapeutic technique that uses a held-eye position to access the neural pathway within your brain that holds a specific memory, trauma, or emotion. It allows you brain to process that event without you necessarily having to talk about it. Brainspotting allows processing by bypassing the conscious mind and accessing the deeper, subconscious mind.

In a brainspotting session, the practitioner will focus more on your body sensation and how a memory is showing up for you in your body. For instance, when people experience anxiety, they often report a tightness in the chest or labored breathing. In a brainspotting session, the therapist will focus on the increasing or decreasing of the tightness in the chest while your brain is actually processing the trauma that creates the anxiety in the first place. This technique is affecting a wide variety of emotional and somatic conditions. Though brainspotting has been shown to be an effective trauma treatment, it can also be beneficial in enhancing performance and creativity.

# AMBER'S STORY
## A Day like No Other

On November 8, 2018, my mom woke me up like any other day. I got dressed and ready for school and we looked outside. It looked and smelled smoky. We didn't really think about it that much because fires happened around there all the time. It wasn't really a big deal. Also, when I was pretty young, two or four, we had to evacuate the area, but the fire didn't burn down anything. We got in the car and drove to school. My dad left early that morning to go to a conference in Sacramento. He was safe. My mom dropped me and my sister off at school, and she went to work.

When I got to school, I did what I normally did. I put my backpack down by my classroom, and I went down to the blacktop to play basketball with my friends. It started to get really dark and smoky. There were ashes falling from the sky and huge pieces of burned wood. The yard duty personnel and teachers called us back inside and we sat down. They told us to get our phones and call our parents. I used the teacher's phone to call my mom and let her know everyone was getting evacuated.

Earlier that morning, my mom told us if anything happened to go to my third-grade teacher because he would take care of us. My mom had to take care of our dogs and horses. We waited for our teacher to come back to us in his classroom while he helped other students. Once he got back, my brother and I went to his car in the parking lot. There was some traffic there, but once we hit the road it got super bad, and we sat in traffic for five hours or so. At first, when we got in his car, I was crying because I was super scared. I wanted to make sure my horses and family were OK.

The cell service wasn't very good. I couldn't talk to my mom, dad, or sister. My brother was crying. Our teacher was calming us down and telling us jokes so we would stop crying. I could tell he was scared, too, but he was hiding it so it wouldn't scare us more. The traffic started to move and I ate some stuff I had in my backpack. I started coloring to occupy my mind. We finally got ahold of my mom. She told us she had the dogs and was getting all the horses loaded. She couldn't find our cat. We had to leave her behind. I started crying. She also told us that her sister was with one of her coworkers and that she was OK.

We were still stuck in traffic and the car filled up with smoke. I was coughing. I had trouble breathing. We got to the end of Paradise into Chico and there were fires on both sides of the road. We were surrounded by it. Some people were walking behind us. We saw a guy who worked at our school, and we offered him a ride. He said he would get to Chico faster and safer by walking. It started to get hotter because there were fires everywhere. Things were melting and falling over right next to the car. I didn't think I was going to make it because fire was so close.

A little bit after, we made it to Chico. The traffic was light. Our teacher took us to where his family was staying with a friend. I was still crying about my cat. His wife helped me calm down. We finally got a call from my mom. She told us she got all six horses and all the dogs.

We went to a church where people were finding their parents. It was basically a regrouping center. That's where my sister and I met. Then we went to where our neighbors were staying. They had a safe place where we could stay.

My mom ended up in Oroville with our pets. A friend of the family picked us up and drove us to another church where my mom was staying. We met my mom and dad and stayed at their friend's house for a couple of days. The fire shifted ways and it started to head toward Oroville. It got smokier and smokier, and we had to get out of that place. We went to a horse therapy place. All the horses were there. We went to load them up and leave, but my horse wouldn't load in the trailer. I was crying and worrying about the horse, but we had to leave.

We went to Auburn and my horse stayed somewhere safer. We stayed with my dad's old coworker. We had all our dogs and bunnies, but we had to leave our chickens. We stayed there for a couple of nights. When we left there, we went to Wheatland where we met my dad's current coworker. We were going to stay in a tent. We could use their showers and have our horses. It was a perfect long-term setup, but we ended up leaving because they smoked. I was already sick from all the smoke I had inhaled. We went to my dad's work in Sacramento. We hung out at my dad's office with his coworker who gave us some blankets and Spam. I ended up liking the Spam because it was the only thing we had to eat. My dad's other coworker called and offered to let us stay at his place because he had enough space. We went there and had dinner, took showers, and we stayed there for three months. They are like family to us now. If they weren't there, we wouldn't know what to do.

# Amber's Reflections

*Looking back, what was the worst part of it for you?*

When we were surrounded by the fires, because in my head if I were going out now, there is so much stuff I could've done. I couldn't do anything at the moment. I was helpless. It was super scary.

*If you could have done anything differently, what would you have done?*

Probably when I woke up, I would have told my friends they needed to evacuate and grab all the important sentimental stuff. I wouldn't have gone to school, so we wouldn't have to look at the fires and have that life experience of scariness.

*What have you learned going through this experience?*

I learned that you can definitely rely on other people, and you can see who is really on your side going through something like that.

*Where do you feel like you are still struggling, or where do you feel stuck, if you are?*

School and the memories of it. I started to have anxiety and panic attacks. The first one I had, I was dreaming about the fire, and I felt like I was dying. The stress of school got to me, and I started to have panic attacks all the time.

### What keeps you going?

My friends. They are so awesome. They understand it and they are better than the ones I had before the fire.

### If you could give another survivor any advice, what would you say?

I'm glad you're alive and you're healthy. Remember you can confide in other people because they can really help you!

# Clinician's Corner
# Dream Processing and Your
# Subconscious Mind

It is common for those who suffer from PTSD and other effects of trauma to have vivid dreams and nightmares about or related to the trauma. Nightmares are one of the many symptoms of posttraumatic stress disorder. According to the Diagnostic and Statistical Manual of Mental Disorders, Fifth Edition, or DSM-5 for short, nightmares are classified under PTSD Criterion B, which discusses intrusive symptoms associated with PTSD. Other symptoms include unwanted upsetting memories, flashbacks, physical reactivity, and emotional distress.

Recurrent nightmares are a central feature of posttraumatic stress disorder (PTSD) among both military combat veterans and trauma-exposed civilians (Germain, A., 2013). While the majority of individuals afflicted with PTSD experience sleep dysfunction, the prevalence of posttraumatic nightmares in patients with PTSD can be as high as 72% (Leskin, GA., et al.)

While dreams and nightmares are disturbing at times, they are a way for our minds to work through trauma and for our brains to make connections more efficiently (Hartmann, 1996). Dreams and nightmares represent mental and emotional processing within the trauma centers of our brain, the amygdala. Our conscious mind will often block out and repress trauma because the brain registers it as too painful or too overwhelming, but the information still needs to be processed.

As we sleep, our brains take that opportunity to try to relieve us from the trauma by processing it through dreams and nightmares. Many clinicians who work with dream interpretation can help a client decipher meanings of their dreams and nightmares in order to rationalize and understand what they are needing to heal from. Dreams often reflect the world we see and feel when we are awake (Newsom, 2020). How does one work through unwanted trauma, dreams, and nightmares? The following section is meant to be a guide to help you accept, understand, and manage the nightmares associated with your trauma. It is always recommended that you seek a mental health professional to help you make sense of your nightmares. An outside perspective can help bring new reasoning and logic to what you are experiencing.

It can be helpful to keep a journal or log of your nightmares. This can help track how often they occur, if they are recurring, if there are any common themes in your nightmares, and any other information your brain wants you to know. A mental health professional can help you process and find meaning with the information from the log. A Dream Log can be found on the resources page here:

www.SiftingThroughTheAshesResources.com

Other practices you and your therapist can develop are self-soothing skills and healthy coping mechanisms to utilize when you experience a nightmare. These self-soothing and anxiety-reducing techniques can be performed before you go to bed and if/when you wake from a nightmare in the middle of the night. Some examples of these self-soothing tools include taking a bubble bath or shower, reading a book to distract your mind, visualizing a safe space, calming meditation, or calling a friend to talk through your anxiety. It can also be helpful to change your environment in order to avoid building a connection between your anxiety and the place you sleep. If you experience repeated nightmares, your bed, bedroom, and even the time of evening you go to sleep can become triggers and activate anxiety about having nightmares.

When you wake during the night with a nightmare, try getting up and moving to a different room. This helps your brain move forward, past the nightmare, and helps to distance your reality from your dream experience. Another intervention that can be done with a trained therapist is called Imagery Rehearsal Therapy (IRT). IRT was developed in 1978 by psychiatrist Isaac Marks. This type of therapy can be empowering because, even though you cannot control the types of dreams and nightmares that you have when you are asleep, you can change the way the dreams end while you are awake. For example, in Amber's reflection about her dreams connected to the fire, she stated that she felt like she was dying. In IRT, Amber could change the events of the dream and rewrite the narrative of the dream's story line.

Here is another example of IRT and how it can help you change the neural pathway of the experience in your brain. If you have a dream of being stuck in the house while the fire was moving closer to you, you could change the ending of the story by visualizing and speaking into existence that you got out of the house and made it to safety. Remind yourself that your brain is trying to heal, and you deserve your own love, grace, and patience. Healing is not always fun or comfortable, but the process is important for you to overcome your trauma and thrive in life. There is information in your dreams that is trying to get your attention about your experience and what your subconscious mind needs in order to heal. Your job is to try to figure out what that is.

# JILL'S STORY
## The Grieving Process

**M**y husband woke up at four in the morning to go to work in Sacramento the day of the fire. I checked to see if school was going to be canceled. The power was supposed to have been turned off on Wednesday evening because a storm was coming. I still would have had to report to work, but I wondered if I would have to get the kids up. I checked my email at 4 a.m. PG&E did not cut the power the night before, and school was on as usual.

My husband left for Sacramento. His territory was Northern California, and he had a company vehicle. He was in transition to be a technical trainer. That day, he was training/teaching a class for technicians. He was commuting somewhere in the greater Northern California area every day. We got up as usual and started getting ready for school, like any normal day.

I got in the car to drive the kids to school. As soon as we got on Pentz Road, we could see the sky looked different. There were fires every year, but this one looked different. We didn't even know there was a fire yet. I told my kids to call their grandma to see if she could see the fire since she lived on the canyon. She confirmed there was a fire. We called my husband to tell him to turn around.

School was still on. I dropped my daughter off and then we went to the school where I worked. When I got to work, the phones were ringing off the hook. It was pretty smoky at that point and there was ash falling. My daughter reminded me that she needed a note to excuse her from PE because of her asthma. I frantically wrote her a note. I put my phone number on it and sent her to school. She walked to school from there.

As soon as I sent her away, I had a bunch of different departments calling me. Teachers called me asking if we were evacuating. I looked at my emails. There was nothing. School was on as usual. Within a matter of minutes, my daughter at Ponderosa Elementary called and told me they were evacuating. I told her to go with a teacher who was our neighbor. I said I would meet her at home as I had to get her horse. Her horse was in the evacuation zone and didn't like to load.

My first thought when she called me was that this would be a regular evacuation like we had before multiple times. I was in my heels and a dress, and I was running out the door. Two of my coworkers came in, and I told them I needed help. One got my daughter. My coworker evacuated the adult school for the severely disabled. I drove to my house to change my clothes, get the three dogs, cat, bunny, and my husband's pills. I left the chickens at the house. I threw my coworker a bag to empty the cupboards.

My neighbor, a retired fire chief, was panicked. I knew if he was panicked, it was bad. He and his wife yelled at me to just get out. I struggled with getting the dogs into the crate, and I couldn't find the bunny carrier. I grabbed a bag, got the bunny, and threw the bunny into the bag. I had a bagful of pills. I momentarily thought the big dog would be OK. She had plenty of water. I thought I didn't need to bring the big dog because she would scare the horses.

The fire marshal was yelling at me to go. So, we threw our bloodhound in the back of the truck, but I couldn't find her leash. I got a rope and tied it around her neck and made my coworker sit in the back of the truck. This was my husband's brand-new truck. We were not allowed to eat in it, and I had two pugs, a bunny in a bag, and a bloodhound in the back. At that point, we were driving toward Pentz Road. We were driving toward the flames.

We boarded our horses at the property of the assistant superintendent of the school. My coworker's daughter had three horses, we had our horse, and another boarder had two horses. There were six horses, total. While I was driving, the assistant superintendent's daughter called me from Cal Poly. It was her birthday, and she was in tears, begging me to get the horses out. We got all of the horses loaded after many struggles with vehicles and tow hardware.

We drove down Pentz Road to Oroville. There was no one on the road—nobody. I looked in my rearview mirror and we were right below the fire line. I talked to both my daughters and my husband on the phone. Both the kids were safe and fine. They were in the process of evacuating. I didn't tell the girls that I couldn't find the cat at the house. I didn't have the cat.

We got to a church in Oroville and got everything unloaded. We got the horses situated. We got the dogs situated. I went to check in with my kids, but the cell towers were down. We watched the news for an hour and a half. The hospital burned. McDonald's was gone. The whole town was gone. I looked at my coworker. The whole town was gone.

I started to panic wondering about my kids. I had no idea where they were. All I knew was the town was gone. I was numb. I looked at my phone—nothing. No texts, nothing. I asked my coworker if he heard from our other coworker, who my daughter was with. He said, "No."

After more than an hour, I finally got a text from the person my youngest daughter was with that simply said, "Safe." Then I focused on my other daughter and husband. Another hour and a half went by. That turned into three hours with no communication. Finally, I got a call, and it was my other coworker with my other daughter. She said, "Your daughter saved our lives."

She told me her whole story of their evacuation and how they got stuck in traffic and how the firefighter ran down the road telling everyone to get out of their cars and run. The flames were going faster than the cars could go, so they got out and got to Chico. I knew my daughters were both safe. I was in Oroville. My daughters were in Chico but separated from each other. We couldn't get from Oroville to Chico because Highway 99 was shut down. I got a call and was told my older daughter was not doing OK. She had gone through the wringer and was lucky to be alive.

I was at my friend's church in Oroville. My girls were in Chico and my husband was still in Sacramento. A stranger offered to get my kids. He said if he could have his kids with him, I should have my kids with me. He was a Paradise person. My daughter got in the car and knew the guy's kids. It is a small town. They were brought to Oroville. I had my kids.

We slept in a person's house—someone from the church—along with thirty other people. My amazing coworker set that up. Then the next day, when I woke up, I could see Paradise burning. I decided to take us all to look. We were in the back of a truck. We were all there grieving. The park ranger told us we couldn't put all the people in the back of the truck, but the pastor calmly walked the ranger away from us. We didn't hear what he was saying.

I later found out he told the ranger to give him a ticket and do what he had to do, but "these people lost everything. They lost all they had." If he could do something to give us peace, then go ahead and give him a ticket. He told the ranger he lived around the corner and would have us back safely in less than two minutes, "but, if you have to give me a ticket, don't let them see." The ranger said, "Get them home safe."

Another friend called, and her nephew was at another church, and they couldn't get him. They knew I was in Oroville. Another friend put on a wild African outfit, and we told the nephew to look for a girl in a super-bright African dress. You couldn't miss her. She was a walking rainbow.

So many things that should not have happened, happened. We got all of the horses out. People we didn't know took care of them for more than a month. Our breeder took care of our dog. We had to have other people take care of our horse, too. We lost the cat in the fire, and we had to give our horse away. Our hound passed away. She was never the same after the fire. Her anxiety was so bad she broke windows in the barn. She was hit by a car and had hip and lung injuries. She was severely traumatized and we had to put her down. The losses are never-ending. How long is my train, where is the caboose?

# Jill's Reflections

### What was the worst part of the experience for you that day?

There are two worst parts. During the experience, not having communications with my kids—not knowing if they were safe, not knowing where they were. It was an absolutely gut-wrenching feeling. Then, after, the hardest part is the loss of what we had and the loss of the community. We chose not to rebuild. We chose not to go back to Paradise. I didn't want my oldest daughter to have to re-experience driving through town.

### If you could have done anything differently, what would you have done?

I ask myself that question every day, and at the end of the day, we are all alive. We know we are so much stronger than we thought we ever were, and we have met some amazing people we might have never met.

### What have you learned from going through this experience?

Being OK. My positive attitude at the school district was helping people in need. I was always that person helping—the gift of giving. Standing in line to get free pet supplies because my pets didn't have food. I was thankful to whoever donated. I had to think, "OK, it is my turn." Everything changed in the matter of an hour. Just have compassion for people because things can happen so fast, and you are in a situation that you never thought you would be in.

### Where do you feel that you are still struggling or stuck?

I want to go home. It is not there. Even if I rebuilt it, it would never be the same. So many people are not there. It is not the same. I grieve that whole loss.

### What keeps you going?

My kids. I have to get up, put a smile on my face, and have some sense of normalcy. I have kids, pets, and a husband. People depend on me.

### If you could give another survivor any advice, what would you say?

I know the pain. I understand the pain. Give yourself permission to not be OK. And give yourself permission to take the time to heal and ask for help. It is a part of you, and it takes a lifetime to recover from it. It is a grieving process. We take each day one day at a time. Take care of yourself. Be able to know when to ask for help.

# Clinician's Corner
# Boundaries and Giving
# Yourself Permission

There is a very important aspect to not only healing from trauma but bringing balance back into your life: *permission*. Permission to heal, permission to grieve, permission to breathe, permission to fall apart and not be OK. It is OK to not be OK. Hear that again. It is OK to not be OK.

We are often pressured by our society, our culture, and even by our own family to push past the pain and "let it go." In this attempt to "get over it," we essentially tell ourselves that what we are feeling or experiencing is not OK, and that we have to do better or be better because that is what the outside world expects us to do. When you push away the thoughts and emotions you struggle with in an attempt to meet a perceived expectation of healing, you end up abandoning yourself in the process of pleasing others (society, culture, family, or any other outside opinion).

We often learned to abandon ourselves due to early-childhood events that would have made us responsible for our caretakers' needs, physically or emotionally. Therefore, we learned that the other person's needs came before ours, even if we were the child. Perhaps our own parent had a substance abuse problem. Maybe we saw our parents fight and divorce and felt like we had to fix it for them. Maybe our parents had their own mental or emotional struggles, and they placed that burden on us as children. Whatever the situation, we learned that our needs came last. This can have a significant effect on us as adults.

As adults, we tend to be people pleasers in our everyday life. We take on more responsibility than we should as a way to show that we have value. Again, this is a subconscious conditioning picked up from when we were young. We tend to have little to no boundaries with others. We tend to be highly critical of our own achievements. We are perfectionists, over-doers, over-givers, and we forget to love ourselves in the same way we love others. This is where boundaries come in. Boundaries are the sweet sauce that makes our relationships with others and the relationship with ourselves healthy and balanced.

Boundaries are the parameters that tell others how we expect to be treated and what we will or will not tolerate. Boundaries are important. Without them, we can turn into the "doormats" of others or the "walk all over" of others. Having boundaries with ourselves is even more important. How can you set boundaries with others if you have no clue what your own personal boundaries for yourself are?

Personal boundaries can come in all shapes and sizes and are dependent on you and your values. According to Michael G. Quirke, MFT at San Francisco Therapy, setting healthy boundaries is an integral part of living a healthy life. Boundaries protect you. They also help you form your own identity. Only you get to decide what your beliefs, values, thoughts, and choices are. The people around you must know how you define "acceptable" and "unacceptable." By setting healthy boundaries, you are broadcasting your needs and what feels important to you. The following are examples of boundaries that may help accelerate your growth:

- Leaving work at the time you clock off

- Turning off your phone when you are with family

- Saying no when you want to say no

- Staying home when you feel you need rest

- Removing toxic people from your life (some may be family)

- Letting go of things that no longer serve you

The following are examples of situations that may arise from a lack of boundaries:

- Staying at a job that makes you unhappy or staying in a relationship that makes you unhappy

- Overscheduling yourself

- Neglecting your physical or mental health needs

- Talking poorly to yourself

- Putting others' needs above your own more often than not

We want to emphasize boundaries in relation to trauma and healing from trauma. Putting your needs first is not a selfish act. In fact, it is one of the least selfish things you can do for others. You cannot pour from an empty cup. If you do not take care of yourself first, you will be unable to care for others. Think of it this way: those other people you care for also need you to take care of yourself.

So, what do boundaries for yourself look like? Here is a small list of examples that may inspire you to tell yourself, *You matter.* Use this list to start. You may add boundaries that feel more aligned with your personal values and subtract those that do not apply.

- Getting eight hours sleep

- Eating healthy foods

- Prioritizing exercise or increased body movement

- Saying no when you want to say no

- Getting a massage or spa treatment

- Reading for pleasure

- Taking a rest day

- Declining an invitation if you want to stay home

You should also focus on giving yourself permission to take care of yourself. It is so important to allow ourselves the time, space, and opportunities to heal, recover, and find a new normal after we experience trauma. Sometimes, clients come into our office and feel a great sense of relief when we, as clinicians, give them permission to feel. It can sometimes be a defining moment for them in their process. It is as if they need our verbal permission to give themselves permission. So, right now, as you read this, please let us give you permission to give yourself permission to take care of yourself.

The following statements are meant to serve as agreements with yourself to start putting *you* first. We encourage you to say them aloud as you stand in front of a mirror, looking yourself in the eye. This may feel uncomfortable to some people, and that's OK. When we have learned that our needs do not matter, we can have difficulties when we put ourselves front and center. We just ask for you to do your best.

- I give myself permission to receive my own love and support.

- I give myself permission to receive love and support from others.

- I give myself permission to stop, take a deep breath, and connect back into myself.

- I give myself permission to say no when it feels right.

- I give myself permission to say yes when it feels right.

- I give myself permission to take the time I need to heal.

- I give myself permission to release the responsibilities of others.

- I give myself permission to honor my own values and to put my needs first.

- I give myself permission to not be OK.

We hope you find comfort in these statements and that you feel a little bit of the weight and pressure you carry lifted off your shoulders. You deserve to be free from your trauma and the mental or emotional turmoil it has caused. The beauty of this process is that you get to decide when you are ready to move forward with your life, though it may be difficult at times. You get to decide to do the work to break free from those chains. Allow yourself to cry, rage, and express your feelings when you need to. We give you permission to give yourself permission. As stated by Dr. Kate Truitt (2019), once we can recognize the ways in which we have discounted ourselves and avoided tending to our own needs, we can find the strength and courage it can take to create sustainable change for the better in our lives. This is our hope for you. You can access a Boundaries Checklist on the resources page here:

www.SiftingThroughTheAshesResources.com

# JAN'S STORY
# The Morning of the Nightmare from Hell

**I** got up at five every morning. I was sitting in the TV room looking at the TV and the windows were behind me. I was watching national news, and they were not talking about any fire here.

At about 7 a.m., somehow I learned there was a fire in Pulga. I thought Pulga was about twenty miles away and they would get that out. There would be nothing to it. I didn't realize the wind was blowing 50 mph behind me.

I thought we were OK and got a cup of coffee and went back to watch some more TV. The next thing I knew it was about 7:45 a.m. or something like that. There was a knocking and pounding on the door. It was my neighbor who is a rabbi on Saturday and a Baptist minister on Sunday. They are Messianic Jews. He was pounding on the door. He said, "Get out now, the fire is here!"

And I was like, "What fire?" He told us to do it now.

I looked across the street and my fifteen-year-old neighbor, whom I took to school every day, was there. She went to the Adventist Academy so there was no school bus for her. I looked over and she had her back-pack on and she was running over, terrified. She said,

"Jan, Jan, my mom said to come to you. You will get me out."

She had no way to get out. That girl would have been stranded there because most of the people around me had already left. They probably knew what was going on, but not me. I had ten minutes to pull it all together. I got my neighbor calmed down. My granddaughter was living with me at the time. I had her little Pomeranian dog and had to get him in a crate. I had to find my cats. I got one cat and never found the other cat, my wonderful Matisse. Then there was my wonderful Maltese dog. I don't know what happened to him. I got everybody and grabbed what papers I could. We were out of there at about 8:10 a.m.

Going down Pearson, the fire was on both sides. It was pitch dark and the only thing light at all was headlights. It was very scary. I remember a man running beside us. It took us two hours to get from my house on Cherry Lane to Clark Road.

I told my fifteen-year-old neighbor to roll down the window and tell the man we could take him. We had a seat available. She told him, but he said, "I can't go with you, my two children are at the elementary school." I thought, Oh, my God. He kept running and we couldn't help him. I got to Clark. I wanted to keep going to Chico, but they had traffic control on Clark and Pearson. We went where they told us to go. I was only allowed to go down Clark. Clark was even more on fire. I found out later they shut down Clark ten minutes after we went through there. My neighbor was so brave the whole time.

We went south of Ace Hardware on Clark and I looked ahead. There was a long line of hardly moving traffic. I had literally never seen anything like that in my life. There was a complete arc of fire right over the road and I thought I would have to drive through it. I was watching cars going through, and I thought, Oh, my God. Meanwhile, the fifteen-year-old girl did a great job keeping it together.

Fortunately, whatever cell tower she and her mom were talking on was working. Her mom was at the bottom of Clark Road. My neighbor's mom had already been at work in Oroville and was trying to get back up to help her daughter and they were not letting her. She was going to get out of her car and run up Clark Road, if you can imagine such a thing. Her daughter would have been worse off, but she was able to talk to her mom. I called over and told her mom not to come up Clark Road and to stay right where she was. I said we would eventually get to her. A half hour later we did. They were reunited and that was great.

We were at the gas station, and I was trying to get to Durham/Pentz Roads. All I could do was keep going. I had a friend in Oroville we could go to. I followed the friend in front of me, and we went all over hell and back, to Gridley and back, any way we could. It took us two hours to go to Clark Road to Oroville, which was usually ten minutes away. We finally got to this lady's house in Oroville. I was there with a dog and cat in crates, and they needed to get out for a while. The people there were a very nice couple. I didn't have any clothing, just what I wore out. The woman went to Walmart and bought clothing that night. They rigged up a leash for the dog and cat to go potty. The couple was marvelous.

I didn't know what their address was, or I would have sent a thank-you card. We met up with my neighbor's family in Oroville on Highway 99. The fire was on 99. They drove through the fire and then 99 closed.

It was just horrific. We reunited the dog with my granddaughter. The dog is a therapy dog for her anxiety and they needed to get together sooner rather than later. That was a big help. I had my in-laws; my son had been married to their daughter, but my son died in 1998. My daughter-in-law is now married to another man. They are family.

I've had twenty-two years in hell. My mother died in May 1997 at ninety-two years old. My son was killed six months later. Then, in 2002, I was diagnosed with serious cancer. I went through hell with treatment, both radiation and chemotherapy at the same time. It almost wiped me out. In 2006, my husband had some kind of an episode, maybe spinal meningitis.

In 2008 our house burned to the ground in the Humboldt Fire. We lost everything then. We rebuilt that house, and we lost that to the bank. The bank had some nefarious dealings and went bankrupt. They did terrible things to people.

Unbeknownst to me, my husband was getting dementia. I didn't know at that point. In 2012, I inherited some money from my family. We were able to buy a house again, this time outright, in Paradise. In 2013, my husband died. In 2018, we lost the Paradise house. It has been a tough twenty-two years. My friends say they aren't sure why I am not in the "rubber room."

I tell them I have a lot of faith and that has helped a lot, so here I am. Right after the fire happened, I moved into a trailer (in December). I lived eighteen months in a trailer in the driveway of my in-laws. The only funny thing is my cat was their cat when he was little. My daughter-in-law wanted to keep him, but when the cat was four months old, her husband said no more animals, so I got the cat. I had him a year before the fire. But being back at their house after the fire, I said, "Mike, he's back!" Life in the trailer was difficult with my aches and pains. It was hard, but I did it.

We moved back into my house on the first of April, in 2020. I wanted to rebuild. My daughter was afraid. Two houses have burned down. She felt different about it.

# Jan's Reflections

### What was the worst part of that experience for you?

Driving down Pearson with fire on both sides and the wind whipping hot embers at my car and thinking if my tires caught on fire we were done. It was hard for me because I was responsible for my neighbor. Both of us were scared. I kept telling her it was going to be OK. We would be OK. I had no idea if it was going to be OK, but I had to do that for her. She was white as a sheet. She knew she was going to lose her cat because she couldn't find him before we left the house. That was hurting her—she knew. It was terrifying. I was so helpless. We would sit there for ten to fifteen minutes and then move a foot and sit there another ten or fifteen minutes, over and over again. I was not ready for this.

### What would you have done differently?

I don't know what I would have done. It would have been helpful if the alarm system in Paradise worked. If I would have known about the fire before ten minutes prior to evacuation, it would have been more helpful. They said Cherry Lane burned ten minutes later. Sometime between 8:30 and 9 a.m., my house burned down. I was headed to Clark when my house burned down. Now PG&E has a better system. I wish this had happened before.

**What have you learned from this experience?**

I learned I have to be strong and have to face and cope with whatever I am left with. In my case, I was left with nothing. I have to have a lot of faith that things are going to be better. I learned I am going to get some help from the "Big Guy" (pointing up to the sky to indicate God). I have been through this before, so in some way it was helpful to me. I knew because of my home burning down before, I could recover. There are a lot of people who might not believe they can recover, but I knew that, and it helped me.

**How have the recent fires affected you?**

That's where my PTSD comes out. It is in good shape until it is re-triggered. I usually can keep it under control. I went outside; it was dark and red, and I panicked. I said, "We have to go." We left with everyone and cats in crates. It scared the crap out of me. Smoke and the red of the sun triggered me. I did not want to lose my antique dolls. I already lost them twice. So, they were loaded in the car along with important papers. There was so much smoke. We evacuated twice. I was panicked. We went to my contractor's house. We were there overnight and went home the next day. I kept thinking I have it all together, and I thought, I am pretty good except when I am triggered, and then I am scared to death.

**What did you learn from this experience?**

I guess I learned I can go through all of this stuff and still be a "badass." That's what my grandson says: "My grandma's a badass." It means I am a good grandma. I have had panic attacks. My friends say I am their hero.

### What are you still struggling with?

The only thing is the possibility of losing it all again. When the wind starts blowing and they turn off the power. I don't want to go through this a third time. I have a hard time with my anxiety. It is under control most of the time, but this has made me afraid. I am scared. I don't like to lose control of my situation. I have never been drunk, so I have never gone there in my life. I like control. Neither one of my parents drank at all. My dad was extremely allergic. I grew up in Amelia Earhart's home where there was a full bar, but never once did I get into alcohol. The bar was for guests.

### What keeps you going?

Lots of things. One of the blessings of this disaster is the fact that I lost everything, including my grandpa's paintings and the rest of my dolls, but I'm still OK. I have been a miniaturist since I was twelve years old. I learned techniques being on set with my dad. He was director of special photographic effects. I spent many hours on sets building miniatures and I learned a lot by watching him. My dad parted the Red Sea for the film, *The Ten Commandments.* He won three Oscars. We lost those in the first fire.

Right now, I have five projects in my workroom. I am making a three-dimensional paper doll, and I just finished building a sandstone house and stable from scratch. I adore doing jigsaw puzzles. My workshop is now attached to the house. Before the fire, I was afraid to go to the workshop at night because it was too dark. Now I can use the shop twenty-four hours a day.

I'm very interested to watch and see what will happen to my grandchildren. So, I want to be around for that. I look at my life sometimes and I have never been bored. I have no idea what it is to be bored. I am having a great time. COVID hasn't made me bored. I did doll repairs. I lost all my supplies, so I don't do that anymore.

### If you could give another survivor any advice, what would it be?

I am part of "The Cherry Lane Gang" group. With COVID, we haven't been able to get together. We were all meeting at Round Table Pizza in Chico. We can't do it now. The last one we had was the first of March in 2020. I got a lot of support from the group. Make sure you have support and things to do to help get you through any disaster.

# Clinician's Corner
# Substance Use and Abuse

Jan's story depicts the severity of loss that many fire survivors have suffered. The fear, pain, and chaos that followed is enough for any person to struggle with. One of Jan's ongoing struggles is the loss of control she has over herself and her anxiety. As she tells us, she has never been a drinker because she doesn't like to lose control of a situation. Her parents were also not drinkers.

Trauma is often linked to substance use and abuse as a means to cope with the overwhelming and intense emotions that come from trauma and numb the pain and confusion. Addiction can often result from this because, as the body learns its tolerance for the substance, it requires more and more of the substance in order to live with the feeling of being overwhelmed. According to The Substance Abuse and Mental Health Services Administration (SAMHSA, 2021), trauma is defined as any event or set of circumstances that is experienced by an individual as life-threatening or emotionally or physically harmful. From this definition, Pyramid Healthcare (2018) puts emphasis on the phrase "experienced by." Each person's experience is perceived through the lens of that person. This means that one person's trauma may be different in severity from another person's trauma.

This is important to understand because there is often stigma assigned to substance use and abuse. Since trauma comes in many different forms and in various levels of severity, it would be irresponsible to assume that all addiction or substance abuse is the same. Substance use is a form of coping with the internal wounds of trauma, so each survivor's level of resiliency will differ as well. Family history and genetics, childhood trauma, past substance use, pre-existing mental health condition all play a role in how a person may or may not cope with trauma and whether or not they are more prone to substance use or abuse (Pyramid Healthcare, Rehab After Work, 2018).

So, what are the signs of substance use and abuse in someone who may be struggling with trauma or the psychological residual effects of past trauma? According to Lesser (2021), signs of substance use and abuse can look different for each person. We have included, in the following list, the more common signs you can observe either in yourself or in a loved one who struggles with trauma.

- A need to utilize a substance routinely
- Failed attempts at halting the utilization of a substance
- Difficulties with finances because of substance use
- Participating in unsafe or dangerous practices while affected by a substance
- Commitment in things that are unusual, similar to burglary, lying, or prostitution to acquire the medication
- An evasion of things that don't include the individual substance
- Decreased work performance due to a substance
- Relational issues with friends and family due to a substance

- Physical appearance or hygiene starts to deteriorate

- Obvious intoxication or impairment

- Decreased sleep or abnormal sleep patterns

- Heightened anxiety or depression

- Overall change in conduct and temperament (more aggressive, moody, irritable, etc.)

Research has shown a link between early-childhood trauma and the likelihood of an individual using substances as a means to cope with trauma in their adult experience. Lesser (2021) explains that early-life trauma can increase the vulnerability of a person to use substances. He adds that approximately 25% of children and teenagers have had abuse of some kind.

If you have early-life trauma or feel you may have a substance abuse problem, the best course of action is to give yourself grace and love. Your nervous system is heightened. Unless you have healthy coping tools at your disposal, your substance use and abuse is your attempt to stay safe. Reaching out for help from friends, family, and even a therapist can help you start to deal with the underlying trauma and learn better coping tools to help you feel better.

If you believe that you are struggling with an addiction, it is strongly recommended that you reach out to your healthcare provider for a health assessment and the necessary recommendations and referrals. Substance use programs and treatment centers are also available. The best way to get connected to these options is to reach out to your medical or mental health professional who can point you in the right direction. There are Alcohol and Substance Use/Abuse resources in the Appendix.

While substance use may be a quick fix to your deeper psychological pain, it is not a sustainable one. Since the psychological pain of the trauma is essentially numbed or masked with the use of a substance, the trauma and emotions surrounding the trauma can, in fact, be exacerbated. When painful emotions are repressed for an extended period of time, they tend to resurface at a much more intense level. To help you understand this concept, imagine that the brakes on your car start to squeal. You can hear them make noise, but you ignore it, turning up the radio to mask the noise. Over time, the noise coming from your brakes gets worse and worse, louder and louder, and you have to turn the radio up even more. Then comes the dreaded grinding you feel under your feet as you try to brake. You finally take your car in and get quotes on a brake job, and now you need new rotors, too.

While this is a real-life application of the point we are trying to prove, this is the same theory behind what happens when you choose to ignore your psychological pain and trauma and attempt to mask it with substance use. We want you to know that we understand your pain and struggle, and we encourage you to seek help. Substance abuse is something you can overcome, heal from, and thrive after. There is a Substance Use/Abuse Symptoms Checklist on the resources page here:
www.SiftingThroughTheAshesResources.com

# NANCY'S STORY
## Car Hopping

**I** was going to school when I heard about a fire on the radio. I called my grandmother to ask her if she saw it because she lives on the canyon side of town. We got to school, and they put us in the gym. Soon we were evacuated by grade. At school, they started calling parents to come pick up the students. My mom's coworker picked me up with her son, and we were going back to her house by Magalia. We never got to her house because the road was on fire. We had to turn around and keep driving.

There were people trying to direct traffic, but it wasn't really working. There was stuff on fire, and they told us to get out and run because the fire was moving faster than the traffic could move.

The cars weren't moving. There were too many on the road. A lot of people started getting out of their cars and running, which made trying to leave more difficult. Cars were parked on the road and people couldn't get through.

My mother's coworker, her son, and I had to get out of the car. Most people were walking by then. The traffic started to move because some people pulled over, so it made the road less clogged. We had to stop a car and jump in to try to escape, but the car got stuck. After that, we got in the back of a truck with a bunch of other people, but it got stuck too.

We then got in a car with some guy who used to work for the fire department. He took us in his car, but he said he was going to stay behind to help. We stopped a solar company car, and the guy wouldn't let us in because he didn't want us sitting on his solar panels. We got in anyway because there were not a lot of cars anymore. That car got stuck too, and we were back to walking again. We were practically the only people on the road. There were no cars, either. Then a truck pulled around the corner and the driver picked us up and took us out of the burning town.

We stopped at the driver's mom's or his brother's or his sister's house or something. Then he took us to In-N-Out Burger in Chico, where we met up with our families. Our family reunited from there. That night, we stayed with people who knew my mom's coworker.

# Nancy's Reflections

**What was the worst part of the experience for you?**

I don't know.

**But if you could look back, was there something that stands out that is just the absolute worst?**

My mom's coworker was kind of not thinking straight. She wanted to drive down the bike path, but we would have gotten stuck there. And she wanted to go back up to Magalia, but we would have gotten trapped there because there was only one road out of Magalia. Her son is autistic, and she had left him behind, so we had to go get him.

**If you could have done anything differently, what would you have done?**

I don't know, because I don't know if it was smart to leave the car because the traffic did start moving eventually. We didn't see the fire catching the cars, but the firefighters were telling us it was and to just get out.

**What have you learned going through this experience?**

People were helpful a lot of the time.

**Where do you feel like you are still struggling or where you are still stuck?**

I don't. I feel better than I did before.

***Can you tell me what helped you feel better?***

My new school has a lot more opportunities. I have more friends.

***If you could give another survivor any advice, what would you say?***

Don't worry about it so much because if you do, then you will just be sad all of the time. Just try to move forward and find things that bring you happiness.

# Clinician's Corner
# Self-Esteem and Moving On

**N**ancy's story is a great example of how powerful it can be to move on to find gold in the new normal. As she states in her reflection, Nancy feels better than she did before the fires. She is at a new school that provides her new opportunities and a new support system of new friends.

When we are ready and have the eyes to see, our darkest times can bring us blessings and gifts from the ashes. Trauma is hard. Healing is hard. Facing thoughts and feelings that are painful is hard. On occasion, we find the strength inside of us to say, "no more." We decide that our trauma is not our identity, and we will not be controlled by our pain anymore. There is a Self-Esteem Checklist on the resources page here: www.SiftingThroughTheAshesResources.com

When we can allow our pain to be released, we usher in new opportunities for growth, healing, abundance, and blessings. You are encouraged to let it be part of your story, not your whole story.

There is a wonderful thing that happens when you start to heal from trauma and take back control of your life. Your confidence and self-esteem skyrocket and you start to believe, truly believe, that you can handle life stressors. We think Nancy said it best:

*Don't worry about it so much because if you do, then you will just be sad all of the time. Just try to move forward and find things that bring you happiness.*

# PHIL'S STORY
## Faith over Fear

Iwoke up at 8:30 a.m. and heard thunder. My wife, Cindy, came by, and I said, "Good, it is raining."

Cindy said, "No, it isn't. It is fire."

I said "What? Oh, this will pass."

We hung out to try and figure out how bad it was. We learned the fire was in Pulga, which was thirty-five miles away. I said, "Oh, don't worry about it; it will never get here." I was wrong.

There was a fire in Paradise ten years earlier, and some homes burned but everyone came back shortly after the evacuation. Many people thought it was going to be the same exact thing. So did I. I thought we shouldn't worry about it. We would be back tomorrow. That was until we started to go out of town and the whole town was burning down.

We made it down to Chico. We stayed at the East Church for the night. I threw a tantrum. I told Cindy we were leaving the area, as I felt they didn't want us there. We went to our daughter's house in Santa Clarita. Sunday morning, I got a picture of where the house used to be. It was gone. That is really the story, and I am sticking with that story.

It was surreal and it wasn't bothering me. I didn't expect it.

I was feeling that I just wanted to get out. I couldn't even remember what I was feeling. It wasn't that I was scared or fearful. I said at one point, "Thank God I paid the insurance," and really, that is it. I wasn't upset because in my mind, in my perception, I didn't believe anything was going to happen. This is the picture that was held in my head. And that is what happened on November 8.

From the beginning, the bottom line, I had never seen a tragedy that didn't have within it lots of blessings. That would be the thing; I would say have faith and everything will be OK.

My wife helped me get through this. She is just a godsend to me. I can't tell you anything else. I don't know. The fire changed everything.

I wished I'd cleaned out the safe. Cindy's ten-year anniversary band—I was searching for my wedding band, and it wasn't found. I was basically looking for a large diamond that we owned, and we couldn't find it, and I gave up looking for it. The pastor came by, and he kept working after I said, "Let's stop looking." He came over and said, "What is this?" He found the wedding band that I spoke of because it was platinum and didn't melt. Platinum requires higher degrees to melt than gold. The gold was gone. Cindy wore it around her neck. There were pieces of sterling silver that had welded into the platinum. It was kind of cute.

It was all going to be OK. Trust in the Lord. I have a faith that is strong. Even in death, I believe that I am going home to a better place.

I saw blessings of people doing for others and going out of their way to be helpful to others. Blessings will come from any tragedy. Don't look back. Looking back is not looking forward. Looking back, you can be wishing at what could have been. It is probably better to just move on.

# Phil's Reflections

### What was the worst part of that experience for you?

The drive across Wagstaff, feeling blasted like a door of a blast furnace opening, and slamming into a wall of smoke. It was pretty scary for me. But after that, nothing else bothered me too much, because it is an attitude of living that I have. I really believe the Lord has me where I am supposed to be at any given moment. Whether I am doing good or bad.

### What would you have done differently?

Left Paradise a little earlier.

### What have you learned from this experience?

That no one can control the future. We don't know what is going to happen.

### How have the recent fires affected you?

Not much other than having to be prepared to leave if necessary. I mean, it was five weeks of bad air quality. It was smoky outside for five weeks. There was a little prayer of thanksgiving once the smoke was gone.

### What did you learn from this experience?

I can't say I learned much about myself at all. It is another moving through another day. It is what it is. I don't know what to say about it.

**What are you still struggling with?**

My poor wife's PTSD. That's really been extremely tough for me.

**What keeps you going?**

Simply my faith in my God. I believe it. I find my God in a baby in a manger, and it has always been there for me. My Catholic monk, we had a long chat. The best thing for me in my Catholic journey is that Cindy stays close to the Lord and that is why we attend a Lutheran church. I am fortunate that it is Lutheran because I still get the sacrament of the Eucharist.

**If you could give another survivor any advice, what would it be?**

I give other survivors advice all the time: have faith; it will get better. The other piece of advice is from *The Best Exotic Marigold Hotel* (movie): Everything will be OK in the end, and if it is not OK, it's simply not. The end.

# Clinician's Corner
# Supporting Family Members

**F**or some people, the process through the trauma is less complicated and more manageable. Phil has anchored his faith, his relationship with God, and the patience of time to heal. As he stated, though, he still finds it tough to see his wife struggle with her PTSD. We not only commend those who have overcome, or are in the process of overcoming, trauma, but we also commend those who hold space for others to heal as well. The following pages have tips and practices you can utilize in helping, supporting, and processing with others who are struggling with anxiety, depression, and PTSD related to trauma.

It can be difficult watching a friend or loved one struggle with anxiety, depression, PTSD, or any other symptoms related to trauma. The first thing many people want to do is help or try to fix the situation for the other person. It is important to recognize that each person's process is specific to them, and through each experience there are opportunities for growth, healing, and overcoming. It is through this process that the person becomes self-empowered, and their true strength can be fortified. If you take over and do it for them, you essentially disempower them and deny them the chance to triumph and thrive. However, that does not mean you cannot be there to support, assist, or facilitate their healing process alongside them.

This is what therapists and counselors do as well: we hold space for a client's processing and facilitate a safe environment for them to heal and validate their experiences and emotions. Within that relationship, we also provide tips, tools, and insights that can help the client feel more in control of their lives. We will walk you through some beneficial tools that can help you support your loved one through PTSD, similar to the way a clinician would walk a client through it.

Many survivors of trauma have the need to talk through the experience as a means of processing it. When a person holds on to their traumatic experience and talks about it, PTSD symptoms then become internalized and the trauma can manifest in more indirect ways in the person's life, such as in a relationship or job problems. One of the first things you can do for a loved one who may be struggling is to use active listening.

Active listening is when you hold the space with the other person to hear, see, and understand their story, their emotions, and their experience. Active listening requires five parts. These five parts, according to Mindtools.com (2021), are as follows:

1. *Pay attention* - Make eye contact and limit distractions. Distractions can often come off as not being interested. This also includes listening from a space of taking in information.

2. *Show that you are listening* - Nodding occasionally or utilizing appropriate facial expressions can convey to the other person that you are tracking with them and that you are hearing them.

3. *Provide feedback* - Ask clarifying questions or make statements of reflection. These can be "What I hear you saying . . . " or "It sounds like you are saying . . ." These are great ways to let the other person know that you are interested in what they are saying.

4. *Hold your judgment* - When a person is feeling vulnerable or uncomfortable in their emotions or in their story, they may fear they are being judged. It is important to allow the other person to finish talking before asking clarifying questions. You do not have to agree with the other person, but you are encouraged to refrain from interrupting them with counterarguments or your own opinion. Let that person have the speaking floor in an emotionally safe space.

5. *Respond appropriately* - It is important to be candid and honest in your responses. It is OK for you to say, "I am not sure what to say, but know that I am here for you if you need me" or "I do not have much experience with this topic, but I can see that you are holding a lot of emotion." If you do have opinions, we suggest asserting them in a respectful and productive manner. Imagine the roles are reversed. How would you want someone to respond to you?

The second thing you can do to support a loved one struggling with PTSD is to validate them and their experience. You want to provide the appropriate form of validation. People often attempt to validate others without actually knowing how to do so. While the intention is pure, the execution may be less than desirable.

Validation is not agreeing with the other person unless you do, in fact, agree with them. Validation is saying that (even if you don't agree with them) you can understand their perspective and can see why they feel the way they do. The following are some validating statements you can use.

- It makes sense that you feel . . .
- It makes sense that you think . . .

- I can see that you were really affected by [event].

- Thank you for being vulnerable and allowing me to hear your story.

- What can I do to help you right now?

- Your emotions make sense to me because . . .

- I value your ability to . . .

- What you are thinking/feeling is normal.

- I wonder if you . . .

- I notice that you . . .

- How are you feeling about . . .

- What happened? (Avoid asking "What is wrong?").

The third and final thing you can do to help someone who is struggling with PTSD is to provide them with empathy. Emotion researchers generally define empathy as the ability to sense other people's emotions, coupled with the ability to imagine what someone else might be thinking or feeling (University of California, Berkeley). In essence, empathy is the ability to put yourself in the shoes of the other person. Again, you do not necessarily have to agree with them, but you can imagine what it is like to be in their shoes. This can help them feel less alone in their experience and in their struggle.

To clarify, having empathy for your loved one is not the same as taking on their struggles as your own. You are encouraged to have strong boundaries with yourself in this way. You are not responsible for healing or fixing the other person. In truth, this is their journey to navigate. You can surely walk alongside them instead of over-connecting to the person's experience and taking on the responsibility to heal them.

These simple yet effective steps can help you support your loved one in their struggle with trauma and PTSD symptoms.

# PART 2:
# The First
# Responders'
# Stories

# The Importance of First Responders

**W**hen tragedy strikes, first responders are the ones on the front lines. Their job entails risking their own safety and well-being to be of service to others. Their "typical" day at work is not like yours or mine. They often experience death and trauma as part of their workday. They then have to continue their shifts and go home to their families and do it all over again the next day. For those who responded to the events of November 8, 2018, this was not going to be a "typical" day, and many did not return home to their families for many, many days. First responders from multiple counties, cities, and states responded to the Camp Fire, and many lived on the battle lines for days and weeks on end.

An estimated 4.6 million people serve as career and volunteer firefighters, police, emergency medical technicians, and paramedics in the United States (US Department of Commerce, 2020).

Professional fire departments protect 70% of the US population with a total of 1,041,200 firefighters serving nationwide (Fahy, R. and Evarts, B., et al, 2020). They often work under extreme conditions such as unpredictable environments, harsh terrain, and limited resources. However difficult the job, they still show up and sacrifice their health and their lives in order to protect the community they serve.

The role of first responders comes with many risks, stressors, and mental health challenges which are intensified by the nature of their job. They face challenges such as abnormal shift schedules, interrupted sleep cycles, disruptions to their family life and work/life balance, witnessing trauma and death, and vicarious posttraumatic stress disorder from being the first to arrive on a scene of an accident or violence. More recently they encounter the stress of being a first responder in a time when there are those in society who are intent on harming them.

The truth is that our communities would not be able to function without first responders. They are the ones you call when you have an emergency or need help. They are the ones who keep us safe when life becomes unsafe, and they play a vital role when a crisis occurs. Who are the first responders? They are your police, sheriff, firefighters, dispatchers, paramedics, EMTs, and hospital emergency room nurses and doctors. They all work together as a lifeline to ensure that the public is as safe as possible. Their stories of the Camp Fire are just as important as the survivors' stories.

**Here are the stories of two first responders.**

# DANA'S STORY
## First Responder-Dispatcher

**I**was asleep at home on November 8, 2018. I was on a graveyard shift from my job as a dispatcher for the Rocklin Police Department. I was kind of removed from the fire because I worked in a different county, but when I woke up, I heard about the Camp Fire.

One of my officers was at one of the hotels and pulled someone over. Their license plate came back to Paradise. One of our volunteers worked for an assisted living facility in Paradise. He and his coworker got their little travel vans and drove to Paradise, against traffic, on the day of the fire to get the people out of the facility. They left in the morning and didn't get home until that night. They spent their entire day transferring patients.

When the Santa Rosa fires happened the year before, we helped the survivors by setting up a store where we collected new items, boxed them up, and drove the items to Santa Rosa. The first responders in Santa Rosa started their own store just for first responders whose houses and extra uniforms were gone. They lost everything. I thought it was a great idea. I presented my thoughts to our police chief.

I started a fundraiser on my Facebook page to reach out for funds to help the survivors. I learned from the year before that survivors first need money, not stuff. People started reaching out to help.

We turned our Emergency Operation Center into a store where people could bring donated items. We set up the whole large room. The middle of the room was clothing of all sizes, for all ages. A lot of stuff was new. We had a screen-printing company that went out of business, and they donated T-shirts and sweatshirts.

By the time the center was all set up, my Facebook fundraiser alone garnered seventeen thousand dollars. The overall message was that people trusted us, and they knew where the money was going. Our total funds raised for the survivors was close to sixty thousand dollars. People would just come in with cash and department store gift cards. It was awesome. I put a message out on our Police Officers Association Facebook page letting people know what was needed, and typically, by the next morning, the items were there. I'd wake up and think it was like little elves were bringing them to us.

The chief's wife basically did everything for me during the day since I worked the graveyard shift. At night, I would try to field all of the social media conversations, which was like a full-time job. People wanted instant answers.

People started bringing us food donations, too. We took fliers to all the hotels, where a lot of the survivors were staying. We told them we were here for them. Being able to do this for all those people was awesome. It made me feel like I was Super Santa Claus. People wanted something, and I got it for them. The survivors began going on Amazon and creating wish lists.

For some people, it wasn't about having shampoo or toothpaste, the littlest things in life. It was about having *your* shampoo and *your* toothpaste, not somebody else's. "I have nothing in the world; I just want Colgate." That's not being selfish.

These people were all, at some point, productive members of society. Just because they were now victims of the fire doesn't mean they shouldn't have their Colgate or whatever was meaningful to them in the wake of the crisis. It was good to create happiness amid the horror.

I was trying to keep it just law enforcement, instead of society, or first responders, because I didn't want a bunch of junk. I don't mean to sound rude, but money is actually more helpful than things because then we could get them what they needed. The stuff that was showing up in Chico by the busload made more work. It was creating an additional disaster. That was not helpful. People felt so freaking helpless. This fire took out a whole town in minutes.

I don't remember how long we stayed in business. I feel like it was almost a month. We had tons of people reaching out to us and it kind of got crazy.

We had "Shop with a Cop," and we got some of the Paradise kids and added them to our group. Normally, we would reach out to the schools and get local people. After all, in January many Paradise kids would be attending our schools.

At some point, one company had some kind of computer thing going on. They would refurbish computers and sell them for fifty dollars apiece or something. They gave me as many as I wanted. I think I ended up with about twenty for the survivors.

People were looking for housing. All the best intentions by those donating furniture such as beds and dressers did not take into account that people didn't have anywhere to live or to store the items until they found more permanent housing. These people were going to become our residents and we wanted to help.

On Christmas, a year after the fire, a woman who had adopted a family of four or five after the Camp Fire reached out to me. She said, "They're still not doing good. They're actually staying with me. Is there any way we could do anything?" So, I did another fundraiser on Facebook. People gave money. I still had some gift cards and cash—about twenty-six dollars. I've just been holding on to it just in case something came up. You never know. We helped that family and got them a bunch of stuff.

Later, we went to deliver some items to a family in Paradise. That was the first time I had seen it since the fire. It was crazy. For a while thereafter, every day or every week, somebody was bringing us something. There were warm home-baked cookies, bagels, and lunches. I was amazed.

A woman called and wanted to thank us for our actions by giving us money. I explained we couldn't take her money as we are a government agency. She ended up getting our whole department lunch the following week. When I met her, we shared a tearful hug. I realized she was from Paradise. Her family had relocated to Rocklin after the fire.

That's pretty much how that ended. That's how the Camp Fire ended for me.

# Dana's Reflections

### What prompted your involvement as a helper?

I was working the graveyard shift during the fire. I noticed a large influx of survivors in our area. At first, we were going to gather supplies and take them to the affected area. But as more information was gained, we realized it was unrealistic to do that.

### What was the most meaningful part of being a helper through this disaster?

The most meaningful part of helping was the amount of people we were able to help. I think, when it was all said and done, we helped about five hundred families. We welcomed them into our community and helped them gain a new sense of "community."

### How did the fire affect you as a helper?

The situation had a very emotional impact. Watching the news, hearing survivor stories, and seeing first-hand the look of relief was very overwhelming. We had to stay strong for them, but with each story the impact was harder and harder.

### What was the hardest or most challenging part of being a helper?

The hardest part of being a helper was feeling like you weren't doing enough. I worked graveyard and had to rely on a lot of great helpers. I basically kept the information flowing to my group. While I was sleeping, they would make sure we had enough supplies, reach out for additional helpers, and support the survivors.

### What have you learned about yourself going through the process?

I mostly learned that I can be a great leader. When I see a need, I figure it out and make things happen. Because of working graveyard, I learned that I can let things go and if you have a strong team, you can accomplish anything.

### If you had any advice you could give a helper, what would it be?

My advice would be to have a strong support system and know your role.

# NEIL'S STORY
## First Responder-Firefighter

It was my normal shift at the firehouse station in El Dorado County. It was a hot, windy day. We knew the winds were coming, and we knew it was going to be a bad day. I am at a firehouse that has an OES [Office of Emergency Services] grass rig which was meant to go out of the county. You choose to work at a firehouse like this because you know you are picked to go out of county for these fires.

The crew I was with, the three of us have under five years of experience, and the captain I was with had twenty years in the fire department. All of us younger firefighters are big into social media. Right away we were getting social media things firing up about Magalia, Paradise, high winds, and things are spreading quickly. Right when that was happening, I started sending text messages to my wife saying, "Hey, just letting you know we might be going up soon; it is around the corner." We kept getting messages that crews were already being sent up from Roseville and Rocklin, and I'm thinking, all right, we are up next.

Then all of a sudden it was a lot of "Houses are burning, people are stuck," and "Everyone's getting sent, our bags are getting thrown on the rig, and we are leaving." There were five engines on a strike team from other fire departments, one strike-team leader, and an assistant strike-team leader, so there were two guys. And our fire engines are the Type 3 brush trucks, so they are four-wheel, off-road, big-lifted trucks. We all met at a Safeway off I-5. A strike team meets at one area, and we all go together because when all five of the rigs are together, we are more efficient. That's what they call a strike team.

When we got to the rendezvous, the two chiefs said, "All right, this is what we're going into." We were already seeing the dry column of smoke from our meet-up point, and we were like, "Wow, this is big." We are seeing on social media that people are evacuating. We get on the road, start heading up there, and we are talking on our channel about trying to figure out what we are going to do and what our assignment will be.

We went to Butte College and got staged till we got an assignment, and we were just starting to realize, from Butte College you could already see the hillside on fire and the sky was blacked out. I've never seen anything like it, and it was noon. It was already, like, I haven't seen anything start this quickly and get established this quickly, and one thing we are hearing is that aircraft can't get in because of how windy it is, and we know that's really bad because aircraft is the only thing that can stop these fires and get out in front of them.

We start hearing about the evacuation orders, so we all know there's two ways out—Honey Run and Skyway. We got assigned to Honey Run, which is in the canyon down below Skyway. There's a church at the split, and we're like, "All right, fire is in the canyon; we need to try to evacuate as many people as possible." We were going to go up to Skyway, but everyone was stuck on Skyway there so no rigs could get in, no traffic could get out, and there was no way we were going to get up on Skyway. That's why they sent us down to

Honey Run, where they knew it was very narrow, a lot of overstory [the highest layer of vegetation in a forest, usually forming the canopy].

So, we get down to Honey Run, we back into houses, and we start prepping—clearing brush, trying to do what we can to turn off people's propane—and some people won't leave. They are sitting in their living room saying, "There's fires that have been here before and never got to our house, and we aren't worried about it because we are at the end of the canyon."

Other people are trying to box things up in their car real quick and get out, but it's just a big traffic jam, so we back in to multiple houses. The chiefs—they were in an SUV—said, "We are going to go up ahead and try to evacuate farther up Honey Run. We will let you know what we have and if we have any work up there." And I was like, all right, sounds good.

So, the chiefs take off and start doing their evacuations over their intercoms. Farther up, they turn around. At this point we're looking at Honey Run and both sides of the canyon are on fire. It is steady 40 mph winds. Me and my captain are ten feet away from each other and we can't hear each other. It's so loud it sounds like a freight train, and at this point we have things called trigger points. That means when things start getting heavy, we're like, all right, we either need to back out, and it sounds bad, but let the fire go through and then re-engage, or we need to figure out our safety zones and things like that.

So, at this point, our captain is like, trees were crowning, so they are torching off whole oak trees, spots that were about a mile in front of the fire. Our chiefs are saying fire is down on both sides of Honey Run, both sides of the canyon, we are not going to do anything here. It's going to go right through us, so the chiefs told us to get back to our safety zone.

As three trucks pull out, our chief all of a sudden shouts, "MAYDAY! There is a huge tree across the roadway. We are stuck."

The chief called for resources to help him cut up the tree so he could get past, and pretty much, fire is on his heels. We can't turn around on this two-lane road, so two engines go down there to help him as the rest of us go back to the safety zone.

We are now losing radio communications because the radio towers are burning up. We are exiting the canyon, and we're not going to be able to hear anything. Two chiefs I've known for five years, and it's the first time in my life I've heard a Mayday go out. These guys are not only part of our strike team, they have also taught me in my academy, and things are starting to get a little more personal and it's getting real, fast.

The last thing we hear is those engines get to the tree. They cut the tree, and they say to the chiefs, "All right, you guys, it's time to leave. Where are you?" And the chiefs say, "We are by the tree," and the guys in the two engines say, "No you're not."

Well, there were multiple trees down; they just cut down one tree that was across the roadway, and it wasn't the tree where they were stuck.

So, the chiefs say, "OK, it's time to take off on foot." They grab their wet gear, wildland gear, and they head down the road on foot until they see a minivan that's in the roadway. The lady in the minivan is frozen, stuck in her car and doesn't know what to do. My chief hops in the driver's seat and is like, "We need to leave," and the lady is freaked out. The other chief hops in the back of the minivan with all of the lady's animals and pushes the animals aside. They take off down Honey Run, meet up with the engines, and keep going down Honey Run. Meanwhile, both sides of the road are on fire; there are embers across the road and you can barely see.

We waited for probably forty-five minutes till we got to see them at the safety zone—no radio or nothing. We were sitting there thinking, should we go back? Should we help them or are we going to be a hindrance getting out there? You don't want to be a part of the problem; you want to be a part of the solution. And then once they get back, you know, their car is gone—a one-hundred-thousand-dollar SUV with all the fire equipment in it is gone—all personal equipment, everything they had is gone, and now they are sitting in engines and we're like, we still have to go to work now. Because at this point, it's not like oh, man, an accident happened, we need to get regrouped. No. People are still dying, houses are still burning down; we have things to do.

We retreated to Highway 99 to start the backburn. We went all the way back to 99 and started the burning operations—light the ground on fire all the way around a community that's right off of Highway 99. We start the backburn, and it slows down the progression of the fire going into Chico. We now need to drive back into Honey Run, and it looks like a bomb went off when we go back. Some houses are on fire, some houses are not. There are power lines across the road, trees across the road. People are running down the street—there are cars on fire on the side of the road that I don't know if they are abandoned, I don't know if there are people in them, I don't know if there are people in the houses. I don't know what's going on.

So, at this time, we are trying to put out houses that are partially on fire, trying to protect houses where the fire is getting close to them, and we're trying to just keep everything at bay. During this first period, we have now been awake for forty-eight hours doing this. Usually, you go twenty-five hours doing this, and that's normal. Now you're trying to do your best for as long as possible. We are eating when we can, drinking water when we can, but toward the end of it, adrenaline is now depleted, you have a rocking headache, you've been breathing smoke for the last forty-eight hours. You're just so saturated, and you really don't have a moment to take it in yet. I don't think I fully took all this in until way after the fact.

As we are going through all this, we just can't figure out the state of the matter. We are hearing all these death accounts. We don't know the severity of everything that is going on—they were saying there were hundreds of people that were dead. We're seeing other strike teams on other crews who are saying everything is gone, Paradise is gone, the hospital is gone, everything is wiped out.

But all this is going on, and now it's been forty-eight hours without sleep. You feel like crap, you feel nauseated, all you want to do mainly is call home and tell them you are all right. I think that's what my wife is worried about, if I am all right, because she's hearing all of this back at home. All of our families are hearing this. There's no cell service, she hasn't heard from me in thirty-six to forty-eight hours, and all they know is there are fire engines that have burned, there are people who have died, and she is hearing the worst of the worst on the news. With all this, we finally get to go to base camp, and we finally get to bed down.

Fast forward. After this, it's kind of like a time warp. We were up there for a total of sixteen days, and I'm just now getting a day-one text message from one of my best friends that I work with, that I've known for years. He sends me a text message saying, "Hey, my dad's house is on Honey Run. Do you know if it's still standing?" I'm sitting there telling him, "I don't know if anything has made it on Honey Run." For the next couple days, we are mopping up, meaning we are putting out small fires, but we're also counting structures and seeing what houses may or may not have bodies in them, things like that. Going there and trying to be, like, all right, I am now going to try and find your dad's address, and I am going to tell you if one of your childhood homes that you grew up in is on the ground or not. His dad's house was one of the houses that did survive.

After that, it was kind of like a time warp going through it because, as we know, fire burns really hard for forty-eight hours and then it's kind of just smoldering rubble after that. And after that, I don't know, it was eerie driving through a town that looked like a bomb went off, where big box stores are burnt to the ground. I think one of the eeriest things was when we were driving down Skyway and there were cars with notices from the sheriff's office saying there's a burnt body inside of it.

The weirdest thing was when we were up in Magalia days later, marking homes that were destroyed. There was a house that was burnt down, slammed down to the foundation. The house was destroyed but the car in the driveway, three days later, is still running. All I could assume is there is someone inside, so what do you do? All their belongings are in their car, it's loaded up ready to leave, but it looks like the moon around you and it's just rubble, and it's like, what do you do?

The person is most likely dead inside, so we notify everyone we are supposed to notify. But it's so weird that they are here. They were trying to leave, and they didn't make it out, and their car is still running.

The car's fender was melted, and the lights were melted, but the car was still running. It's just strange and so hard to make sense of. One house is burnt, and another is not. I think one thing that was super strange up there is that people in Paradise, a lot of people, have been there through generations and generations, and that is all they had.

Then, on our off days, we go down to Chico to the base camp. Sometimes we go and eat out, like Chipotle, because we are sick of eating camp food—the ready to eats—so we go out in the community. It looks like a refugee camp in Chico, whether it's the Walmart parking lot that now has a thousand people in it or all the trailers. Then we go and eat, and the thing that really gets me, and gets me to this day, is people come up to us, giving us hugs and thanking us, knowing their house is burnt down, and they still want to buy me a meal. They have nothing, I have everything, and they still want to give me their last bucks, or whatever they have, knowing they have nothing to go back to. I am like, "I want to buy *you* a meal," and they are like, "No, that's not going to happen."

I mean, we're sitting there, and what do you do other than give them a hug and say, "I'm sorry." I don't know, it's just a weird feeling. Like obviously I wasn't directly there—who knows how many of their loved ones were lost or if their house burned down, yet they are still wanting to do this for us. You have a connection now with someone you never knew that is life-changing. The community is so tight-knit.

Once we see our chiefs, both are in shock. We want to continue fighting fire, yet everyone out there just had a near-death experience. And it's like, What do you say to a person that happened to? I'm happy to see you? Are you guys OK? He was in charge of all those strike crews, so he needs to get his head back into the game, and we need to re-engage. And it's this whole weird circumstance of all right, where do we go from here? It's not like, all right, we need to sit back and lick our wounds. We need to re-engage. And we are all thinking, could we have done something differently? Like we need to keep working on what we are doing.

This whole thing felt like you were in a war zone, and you wanted to go home so badly. I came home the day before Thanksgiving, and that day it rained all the way home. We passed a search-and-rescue team task force, and for the next twenty-one days they would be in hazmat suits, sifting through to see if they can find bodies. We were told not to touch any of the bodies, but we did see dogs chained up on people's front lawns that were burnt to death. You would see houses where you knew people were inside, and it was just . . . I can't even put into words the feeling; it's just too much.

A year later, I went back. I tried to tell my family everything that was there and what happened. As we drove through Paradise, my eyes welled up with tears. It became real to me that you could put that town on any map of America, but that it is still people's homes, people's livelihoods. The town is never going to be the same. A lot of these people can't rebuild, and that town was so small.

Eighty-five people died, and I am sure everyone in that community knew one of those eighty-five people. It's hard to put into words the feelings that come out of it. To this day, I wouldn't call this the worst call of the worst days of my job, but it was definitely the most intense I've ever had—the volume, the amount of emotion, and the impact of my surroundings.

As I drove through Paradise a year later, I didn't say a word. I just let the feelings be there, and it was such an emotional experience. Seeing people living in trailers in their front yard, sifting through the ashes. The hardest part was seeing the impact it had on the community.

I think it would benefit a lot of first responders, talking about their circumstances, but some people are so hard and calloused. We call it the normalization of deviance where it's just another day at work. The one thing I remember that sticks out is driving through fire on both sides of the canyon and thinking this is the craziest thing I've ever been through, then adjusting my seat and touching the window, and how hot the window was, and thinking, if I am not inside this rig right now, what is going to happen to us? I can only imagine.

I'm sitting here as a firefighter—in better words, I am a tool; you tell me to go to work, and I go to work. And the driver, as our engineer and our supervisor, his job is to get us to the place safely—just the amount of stress, not on me but on the captain, who's supposed to keep us safe, the engineer who is supposed to keep us safe, and I think of my captain who is supposed to keep all of us safe who got stuck, and his rig is burned and gone.

I remember when we went back in, one of the houses was just starting to catch on fire—there were embers that had gotten to the attic—and us running in, kicking down someone's door and trying to run upstairs and put water inside the attic. And then for the next four hours, we didn't have enough water because there wasn't a hydrant system up there. We watched this person's house burn down, and as the attic is burning down, we're trying to run through the house and rip pictures off the wall and trying to grab what we think is important and put out in front. And then we literally just watched this house burn down all the way down to the foundation.

Hundreds of thousands of dollars and however many memories this person has—all right, we are just going to sit there and watch it burn down? What can you do? And I think that's a weird feeling, that you are there to help, but what happens when the help can't help anymore? I don't know. It's a worthless feeling. That fire—it felt like there was no turning point with this fire, where we felt like we were making any kind of progress.

# Clinician's Corner
# Compassion Fatigue

One thing that is observed with first responders and other helping professions including law enforcement, healthcare workers, mental health professionals and other types of "helping" roles, is the concept of compassion fatigue. Compassion fatigue is when those in the helping field become affected as a result of helping others through stress and trauma for any significant length of time. According to Cocker and Joss (2016), compassion fatigue is stress that results from exposure to trauma or extreme stress in other individuals. It can affect a person's physical, emotional, or psychological well-being.

Compassion fatigue differs from burnout. Burnout is usually a result of prolonged overall dissatisfaction. Perhaps you have been working at the same company or doing the same job function without any real drive or desire for it. Maybe you don't take your vacations or supplement your days off with activities you enjoy. Maybe you do not make time for rest and relaxation from your hectic life. These things can and most likely will cause burnout. Burnout is a compounded accumulation of too much *doing* and not enough *being*.

Compassion fatigue is different. There is a secondary stress or trauma that occurs when there is prolonged exposure to watching or hearing about other people's stress, trauma, pain and suffering, overwhelming circumstances, or excessive hours without the adequate balance of self-care, personal processing, and decompression. This is observed in first responders and other helping professions because of the nature of their jobs. As Cocker and Joss (2016) describe, compassion fatigue, if not treated, can influence the standard of patient care and colleague relationships as well as serious mental health conditions such as anxiety, depression, and posttraumatic stress disorder (PTSD).

There are various signs of compassion fatigue that are noticed in those who work in helping professions for any extended period of time without the necessary or proper rest and recharge. **The signs of compassion fatigue are as follows:**

- *Detachment* - Some may experience a significant withdrawal from friendships, family, and other social connections that are typically personally fulfilling.

- *Mood Swings* - Some may experience dramatic shifts in emotions, negative thinking, or unassigned irritability.

- *Anxious or Depressive Feelings* - Compassion fatigue can alter a person's perspective of the world around them. This can lead to anxious or depressive thoughts and feelings.

- *Addiction or Substance Use* - Due to the high level of "feeling" that those in helping professions may experience, especially working with trauma and loss, some will look to substances or addictive activities, such as gambling, as a means to "numb out" or not feel. Prolonged use of these coping mechanisms can lead to a dependency.

- *Physical Illness or Symptoms* - As you have learned earlier, our body holds a lot of our emotional and psychological stress. This can manifest in a number of physiological ways. Some common physical manifestations include headaches, digestive issues, loss or increase of appetite, sleep changes, body aches, weakened immune system, and even unexplainable illness such as a cold or flu-like experience.

Treating compassion fatigue requires the placement of boundaries from the individual in the helping profession. Boundaries are important because they are the invisible line between the person and the environment. Without boundaries, the separation of work and the individual becomes blurred and enmeshed, thus resulting in both burnout and compassion fatigue. Boundaries keep work at work and keep personal aspects personal. We have all heard the saying, "work-life balance." That is exactly what boundaries are. Especially for those who work with trauma, stress, and other people's pain and suffering, it is vital to maintain a boundary between the work they do, and the necessary personal time needed to rest, recharge, and fulfill them intrinsically. It is also important for one to know their own limits.

What are some ways boundaries can be created in order to minimize compassion fatigue and burnout? These boundaries can come in all shapes and sizes depending on the needs of the person. For some, these boundaries may be scheduling vacations on a consistent basis or making sure that they take their days off. For others, these boundaries can be turning off their work phone on weekends or when they are spending time with family. Other boundaries can also incorporate self-care activities, such as going for a run, hitting up a yoga class, or getting a massage. Other forms of self-care boundaries include eating well, getting restful sleep, going to therapy, or making plans with friends. For some, it may mean finding other employment options.

When a person has been exposed to high levels of stress, trauma, pain and suffering, or grief as a part of the nature of their jobs, they may find themself at a crossroads. Many find that the work they do in the helping field is too much or too overwhelming, and they choose to find other options for their careers. While this can seem extreme, it is actually a common solution, and often the healthiest solution for the individual and their families.

# CONCLUSION

*Sifting Through the Ashes* was a labor of love for the Heartstrings Counseling community and therapy team. We devoted a great deal of time gathering stories of the survivors we helped in the aftermath of the Camp Fire in 2018. The reason we wanted to bring the book to light was not just to share the traumatic stories, but to share the transformation that anyone can go through with any traumatic experience in their life. We wanted to bring the first responders, survivors, and therapists together to talk about how someone stuck in trauma and tragedy can move from a state of darkness to light.

The stories we captured are difficult to read and comprehend. Each survivor's story, along with their reflections, is unique. The Clinician's Corner has valuable interventions and tools you can use in your own life, your own trauma, and your own transformation. Our hope for readers like you is that you will uncover new strategies and tips for dealing with any situation in your life, whether it's a horrific tragedy, a natural disaster, loss of a loved one, mental illness, or anything else you might be going through. As professional licensed therapists, we want the world to be a place where people can live their happiest life.

We don't want you to be stuck in trauma. We don't want you to remain a victim. We don't want you to endure PTSD for decades. We want you to heal and move through these experiences in a healthy way. We want to give you hope that you can triumph from tragedy and trauma. That is our goal in our own private practice as well as at Heartstrings Counseling. Whether you choose to come to us for guidance or want to refer to us, we want you to take these lessons and use them in your life. We want you to pass them on, pay it forward, and share this book and insight with your community of family and friends. We want you to suggest people seek therapy and support in their local neighborhood. Although Heartstrings can legally provide counseling only for California residents, this book is for anybody, anywhere. The goal is to seek help wherever you are.

Heartstrings Counseling, Inc. is a 501(c)3 nonprofit agency and our mission is to provide high quality, affordable counseling and educational services to all members of the community. We strive to encourage positive change and personal growth that will brace and sustain the hearts and lives of individuals, couples, families, teens, and children. We currently have a team of sixteen Associate Marriage and Family Therapists and trainees with compassionate hearts. Their desire is to walk alongside you in your life journey on a path to more peace, love, joy, and hope.

Our therapists have been trained as first-responder counselors and treat a wide range of serious clinical problems including PTSD, trauma, anxiety, depression, and substance abuse. Our counselors either have their master's degree in psychology or are in their last year of their master's program. Each therapist is under the direct supervision of a Licensed Marriage and Family

Therapist (Darla Gale), and they meet weekly for group and individual supervision.

Heartstrings Counseling is committed to providing free and low-cost counseling to disaster survivors and first responders. All the profits of *Sifting Through the Ashes* will be allocated specifically for this purpose. We want to ensure survivors and first responders of any disaster are getting the help they need.

Heartstrings Counseling has been featured in a number of media platforms and has received several awards. Please go to https://www.heartstringscounseling.org/camp-fire-survivor-donations if you would like to see us in the news and learn more about what we are doing in California.

Please go to www.heartstringscounseling.org if you are interested in learning more about what Heartstrings Counseling does here in California and/or are interested in donating to support more survivors and low-income residents.

# ABOUT THE AUTHORS

## Darla Gale, LMFT

**D**arla Gale is a Licensed Marriage and Family Therapist and the CEO/Founder of Heartstrings Counseling, Inc. and Darla Gale Counseling, Marriage and Family Therapist, Inc.

Darla graduated from Brandman University and has a master's degree in psychology with an emphasis in marriage and family therapy. She is a trained EMDR

(Eye Movement Desensitization and Reprocessing) therapist and a certified First Responder Counselor. She has also completed the Faith in Crisis Academy training with a specialized focus on trauma. She has a deep desire to provide healing to those who are hurting, to give each individual the resources for positive change, and to help them gain insight and understanding, resulting in a brighter tomorrow.

Darla holds the belief that you cannot change the past, but you can be strengthened by it. One of her favorite quotes is "It's OK to look back into the past; just don't stare." She has experience working with adults, adolescents, and children bound by anxiety, depression, obsession compulsion, ADHD, anger, addiction, grief, and personality disorders. In addition, she works with couples who are experiencing difficulties with conflict, communication, and unhealthy relational patterns.

Darla's therapeutic approach is creative and engaging, as she combines spiritual, mindful, cognitive, and behavioral principles in her process. Darla believes the client-therapist relationship is of the utmost importance. Her goal is to lead individuals on a personal journey of awareness while providing them with hope, empathy, and unconditional positive regard. In her spare time, she enjoys crochet, cross-stitch, reading, kayaking, fishing, boating, and road trips with her husband.

# Alice Rodriguez, LPCC

**A**lice Rodriguez is a Licensed Professional Clinical Counselor (LPCC), Certified Alcohol and Drug Counselor (CADCII), and a certified brainspotting practitioner in California. She is a trauma-informed therapist who helps people identify past and present issues and heal from the issues that prevent them from living their best life. Providing therapy to veterans and first responders is one of her core passions.

Alice strives to provide a safe, nonjudgmental environment where people can recognize their strengths, learn and develop new skills and knowledge, and use these resources to heal and move forward.

# REFERENCES

AADA (2021). Anxiety & Depression Association of America: Facts and Statistics. https://adaa.org/understanding-anxiety/facts-statistics

Ackerman, C. (2017), Positive Psychology How Does Acceptance And Commitment Therapy (ACT) Work? (positivepsychology.com)

American Psychiatric Association (2020) *Posttraumatic Stress Disorder (PTSD)* https://psychiatry.org/patients-families/ptsd

Barbash, E. (2017) *Different Types of Trauma: Small 't' versus Large 'T'* https://www.psychologytoday.com/us/blog/trauma-and-hope/201703/different-types-trauma-small-t-versus-large-t

CDC (2021). *Suicide Prevention.* Retrieved from Center for Disease Control and Prevention: https://www.cdc.gov/suicide/facts/index.html

Cleveland Clinic (2021) How Box Breathing Can Help You Destress https://health.clevelandclinic.org/box-breathing-benefits/

Cocker, F., & Joss, N. (2016). Compassion Fatigue among Healthcare, Emergency and Community Service

Workers: A Systematic Review. *International journal of environmental research and public health, 13*(6), 618. https://doi.org/10.3390/ijerph13060618

Davis, K. (2018, September 25). *How Does Cognitive Behavioral Therapy Work?* Retrieved from Medical News Today: https://www.medicalnewstoday.com/articles/296579

Davis, S. (2022) *The Importance of Anger and Rage* Retrieved from CPTSD Foundation. https://cptsdfoundation.org/2022/05/31/the-importance-of-anger-and-rage/

Dewane, C. (2008). The ABCs of ACT. Social Work Today. Sept/Oct 2008;d Volume 8, No. 5, page 34. The ABCs of ACT — Acceptance and Commitment Therapy (socialworktoday.com)

Fahy, R; Evarts, B; Stein, G. National Fire Protection Agency 2022

https://www.nfpa.org

Foy, C. (2019) The Reasons Your Loved One with PTSD is Self-Isolating

https://fherehab.com/learning/reasons-ptsd-self-isolating/

Fuller, A. (2021). EMDR: From surround-sound technicolor to silent black and white drama. https://www.amyfullerphd.com/emdr-therapy-from-techicolor-trauma-to-black-and-white-drama/

Germain, A. (2013) American Journal of Psychiatry, Sleep Disturbances as the Hallmark of PTSD: Where Are We Now? https://ajp.psychiatryonline.org

Goodtherapy.org (updated 2017) https://www.good-therapy.org/learn-about-therapy/types/somatic-psychotherapy

Hartmann, E. (1996). Outline for a theory on the nature and functions of dreaming. *Dreaming, 6*(2), pp 147-170. https://psycnet.apa.org/buy/1997-38867-005

Insights (2019). *Are you disconnecting or compartmentalizing.* Retrieved 2021, from Insights: https://www.insightsts.com/blog/are-you-disconnecting-or-compartmentalizing

International Society for Traumatic Stress Studies, 2016 Trauma and Relationships https://istss.org/ISTSS_Main/media/Documents/ISTSS_TraumaAndRelationships_FNL.pdf

Jantz, G. (2016). *The Power of Positive Self Talk.* Retrieved from Psychology Today: https://www.psychologytoday.com/us/blog/hope-relationships/201605/the-power-positive-self-talk

Kaufman, S. (2020). *Unraveling the Mindset of Victimhood.* Retrieved from Scientific America: https://www.scientificamerican.com/article/unraveling-the-mindset-of-victimhood/

Kübler-Ross, E. (1969). On Death and Dying

Leahy, R. (2021, April 12). *How to overcome hopelessness.* Retrieved from Psychology Today: https://www.psychologytoday.com/us/blog/anxiety-files/202104/how-overcome-hopelessness

Leahy, R. et al (2012) Treatment Plans and Interventions for Depression and Anxiety Disorders https://i-cbt.org.ua/wp-content/uploads/2017/12/

Robert-L.-Leahy-Stephen-J.-F.-Holland-Lata-K.-Mc-Ginn-Treatment-Plans-and-Interventions-for-Depression-and-Anxiety-Disorders.pdf

Leonard, 2019). https://www.medicalnewstoday.com/articles/325578

Leskin, G.A., Woodward, S.H., et. al. Effects of Comorbid Diagnoses on Sleep Disturbance in PTSD. *Journal of Psychiatric Research.* 2002;36(6):449–452. [PubMed] [Google Scholar] Effects of comorbid diagnoses on sleep disturbance in PTSD - PubMed (nih.gov)

Lesser, B. (2021). Addiction to drugs and psychological trauma. Dualdiagnosis.org. www.dualdiagnosis.org/psychological-trauma-drug-addiction/

Mayo Clinic (2021). *Complicated Grief.* Retrieved from Mayo Clinic: https://www.mayoclinic.org/diseases-conditions/complicated-grief/symptoms-causes/syc-20360374 Mayo Clinic. (2021).

Mayo Clinic, Anxiety disorders. www.mayoclinic.org/diseases-conditions/anxiety/symptoms-causes/syc-20350961

Mentalhealth.gov. (2021). *Suicidal Behavior.* Retrieved from MentalHealth.gov: https://www.mentalhealth.gov/what-to-look-for/suicidal-behavior

Mindtools.com. (2021) Active Listening: Hear What People Are Really Saying. Mindtools.com/CommSkll/ActiveListening.htm

https://www.mindtools.com/az4wxv7/active-listening

Moyer, N. (2019). *Amygdala Hijack: When Emotions Take Over.* Retrieved from Healthline: https://www.healthline.com/health/stress/amygdala-hijack

Murray, H. et al (2018). Survivor guilt in a post-traumatic stress disorder clinic sample. Journal of Loss and Trauma, 23, 600–607

National Council for Behavioral Health, The (2022.) *How to Manage Trauma* Infographic https://www.thenationalcouncil.org/wp-content/uploads/2022/08/Trauma-infographic.pdf

National Institute of Mental Health (NIMH), *Depression* https://www.nimh.nih.gov/health/topics/depression

Newsom, R. (2020). How trauma affects dreams. Sleep Foundation. https://www.sleepfoundation.org/dreams/how-trauma-can-affect-dreams/

Pollock, A. (2014) When It All Falls Apart: Trauma's Impact on Intimate Relationships https://www.goodtherapy.org/blog/when-it-all-falls-apart-traumas-impact-on-intimate-relationships-0211145

Psychiatry.org (2021) *What Are Anxiety Disorders?* https://www.psychiatry.org/patients-families/anxiety-disorders/what-are-anxiety-disorders\

Pyramid Healthcare, Inc. (2018), Addressing underlying trauma and substance abuse. www.pyramid-healthcarepa.com/addressing-underlying-trauma-substance-abuse/

Pyramid Healthcare, Inc. Rehab After Work (2018). Risk Factors for Substance Use Disorders, 2018. https://rehabafterwork.pyramidhealthcarepa.com/risk-factors-substance-use-disorder

Pyramid Healthcare, Inc., (2018). Addressing Underlying Trauma and Substance Abuse https://www.pyramid-healthcare.com/addressing-underlying-trauma-substance-abuse/

Quirke, M.G. What Trauma Does to Your Ability to Set Healthy Boundaries https://michaelgquirke.com/what-trauma-does-to-your-ability-to-set-healthy-boundaries/

Ready.gov. (2021). *Disasters and Emergencies.* Retrieved from ready.gov: https://www.ready.gov/be-informed

Riopel, L. (2021, February 11). Resilience Skills, Factors and Strategies of the Resilient Person. Retrieved from Positive Psychology: https://positivepsychology.com/resilience-skills/

Rosenthal, M. (2013, November 6). *Living with PTSD and a self-centered lifestyle.* Retrieved from Healthyplace.com: https://www.healthyplace.com/blogs/traumaptsdblog/2013/11/one-u-s-marine-one-guitar-big-impact

Scott, E. (2021, July 8). *How to let go of negativity and stress.* Retrieved from verywellmind.com: https://www.verywellmind.com/how-to-let-go-of-negativity-and-stress-3145006

Substance Abuse and Mental Health Services Administration (SAMHSA) www.store.samhsa.gov/sites/default/files/d7/priv/pep19-01-01-002_0.pdf

Substance Abuse and Mental Health Services Administration (SAMHSA) (2021). Trauma and Violence https://www.samhsa.gov/trauma-violence

Truitt, K. (2019). Self-care after trauma. Trauma Counseling Center of Los Angeles. www.traumacounseling.com/trauma-therapy-blog/self-care-after-trauma/

U.S. Department of Commerce (2020).

https://2017-2021.commerce.gov/news/blog/2020/10/honoring-nations-first-responders.html

U.S. Department of Veteran Affairs, (2021). Anger and Trauma.

https://www.ptsd.va.gov/professional/treat/care/spirituality_trauma.asp

U.S. Department of Veteran Affairs, Mirgain, S. PhD and Singles, J. PsyD (2016), Progressive Muscle Relaxation. https://www.va.gov/WHOLEHEALTHLIBRARY/tools/index.asp

U.S Department of Veteran Affairs. (2021) Sleep Problems in Veterans with PTSD.

https://www.ptsd.va.gov/professional/treat/cooccurring/sleep_problems_vets.asp

University of California, Berkeley, Greater Good Magazine Empathy Definition | What Is Empathy (berkeley.edu)

Van Der Kolk, B. (2014). The body keeps score: Brain, mind, and body in the healing of trauma. New York: Penguin Books.

Veteran Affairs (2021). *Spirituality and Trauma: Professionals Working Together*. Retrieved from U.S. Department of Veteran Affairs: https://www.ptsd.va.gov/professional/treat/care/spirituality_trauma.asp

# APPENDIX

# Crisis and Disaster Relief Information

| | | |
|---|---|---|
| The FEMA Helpline | 1-800-621-3362 | www.fema.gov |
| The American National Red Cross | 1-800-733-2767 | www.redcross.org |
| The Salvation Army | 1-800-725-9005 | www.salvationarmyusa.org |
| Operation USA | 323-413-2353 | www.opusa.org |
| UNICEF | 1-800-367-5437 | www.unicefusa.org |
| Americares | 1-203-658-9500 | www.americares.org |
| Direct Relief | 1-800-676-1638 | www.directrelief.org |
| Convoy of Hope | 1-417-823-8998 | www.convoyofhope.org |
| Samaritan's Purse | 1-828-262-1980 | www.samaritanspurse.org |
| All Hands and Hearts | 1-508-758-8211 | www.allhandsandhearts.org |

# Suicide and Distress Crisis Lines

| | |
|---|---|
| National Suicide Prevention Lifeline | 1-800-273-Talk (8255) |
| Crisis Text Line | 741741 (Text) |
| Suicide and Crisis Lifeline | Dial 988 on your phone |
| Veterans Crisis Line | 1-800-273-8255 (press 1) |
| Veterans Crisis Text Line | 838255 (Text) |
| Military Help Line | 1-888-457-4838 |
| Disaster Distress Helpline | 1-800-985-5990 |
| Suicide.org Crisis Line | 1-800-784-2433 |
| The National Alliance on Mental Illness | 1-800-950-6264 |
| Youth Crisis Line | 1-877-968-8491 |
| Trevor Lifeline | 1-866-488-7386 |
| Trans Lifeline | 1-877-565-8860 |

# Alcohol and Substance Abuse Resources

| | |
|---|---|
| SAMHSA's National Helpline | 1-800-662-4357 |
| Alcoholics Anonymous | 1-212-870-3400 |
| Narcotics Anonymous | 1-818-773-9999 |
| Al-Anon Family Groups | 1-888-425-2666 |
| Partnership to End Addiction | 55753 (Text) |
| National Drug Helpline | 1-844-289-0879 |
| Partnership for Drug-Free Kids | 1-855-378-4373 |
| National Council on Alcoholism and Drug Dependence | 1-800-622-2255 |

# Maps of the Paradise Valley

Maps provided with permission of Butte County, Town of Paradise and Butte County Fire Safe Council.

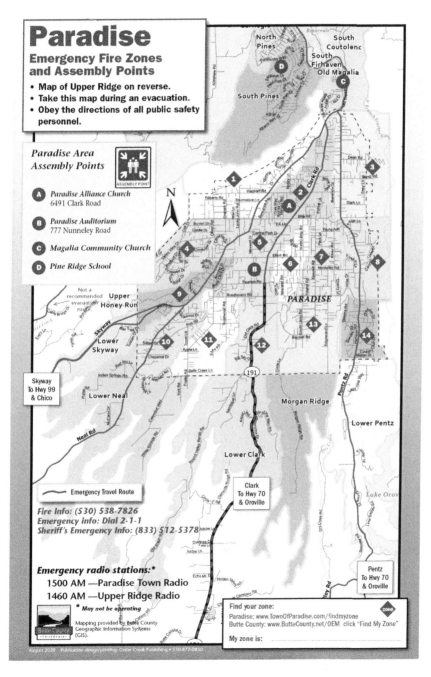

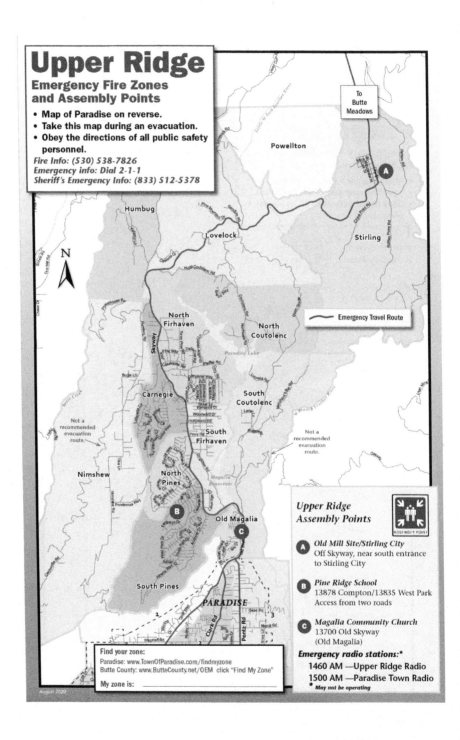

# Upper Ridge

## Emergency Fire Zones and Assembly Points

- Map of Paradise on reverse.
- Take this map during an evacuation.
- Obey the directions of all public safety personnel.

*Fire Info: (530) 538-7826*
*Emergency info: Dial 2-1-1*
*Sheriff's Emergency Info: (833) 512-5378*

To Butte Meadows

Powellton

Humbug

Lovelock

Stirling

N

North Firhaven

North Coutolenc

Emergency Travel Route

Carnegie

South Coutolenc

Not a recommended evacuation route.

South Firhaven

Not a recommended evacuation route.

Nimshew

North Pines

Old Magalia

South Pines

PARADISE

### Upper Ridge Assembly Points

ASSEMBLY POINT

**A** *Old Mill Site/Stirling City*
Off Skyway, near south entrance to Stirling City

**B** *Pine Ridge School*
13878 Compton/13835 West Park
Access from two roads

**C** *Magalia Community Church*
13700 Old Skyway
(Old Magalia)

**Emergency radio stations:***
1460 AM —Upper Ridge Radio
1500 AM —Paradise Town Radio
* *May not be operating*

Find your zone:
Paradise: www.TownOfParadise.com/findmyzone
Butte County: www.ButteCounty.net/OEM click "Find My Zone"

My zone is: _____

August 2020

290

Made in the USA
Las Vegas, NV
04 June 2023

72930102R10167